An Eggcellent

Easter

Francesca Stone

An Eggcellent
Easter

Simple makes, bakes and activities
for the whole family.

POP PRESS

Activities

page 134

Styling

page 164

Introduction

Easter is such a special time of year. The world
is starting to wake up again. Life is bursting
through the cracks of winter's cold, hard shell,
and with it comes an abundance of warmth and
colour. This vibrant time of year feels hopeful
and full of possibility. It's almost as if nature
gives us a fresh new start each year and it's
our job to make the most of it. For me, the best
way to do that is to spend quality time with
my family, celebrating the change of season
and slowing down to notice the magic that
springtime brings.

Our Easter celebrations are packed with
exciting traditions and wholesome activities.
Of course, it wouldn't be Easter without the
sweet treats. Chocolate eggs are an integral

part of celebrating this holiday, but we're not limited to tin-foil-wrapped, simple eggs sold by the dozen in the supermarkets. We can be more creative, even with the humble chocolate egg. At this time of year any sweet or savoury food can be made more fun and whimsical with a little Easter-themed twist. It's the perfect time to throw caution to the wind and sprinkle some joy into our baking.

But it's not just about what happens in the kitchen. This is a wonderful time to bring the family together to enjoy being creative in other areas of our lives. I always over-plan crafts and activities for the holiday; it keeps us busy and makes Easter feel like it's about more than just the chocolate.

The weather around Easter can be very difficult to predict. It can be a beautiful warm spring day, or it can feel like winter will never end, so it's always wise to have activities ready for both outdoor and indoor time. Here in this book I've included many options suitable for wherever you choose to celebrate, whether that is at home, in your garden or in a local park or woodland. Many of the projects in this book are ideal for any space. From decorating eggs and making paper flowers for a fun posy stand, to sourcing from nature to make bunny masks and using recycled materials we all have at home, crafting can bring the magic of spring and Easter alive.

As well as keeping small hands occupied during the time off school, we can also use Easter crafts to decorate our homes. It's the perfect opportunity to add pops of colour and greenery to spaces that need freshening up, by being creative with recycled, foraged or inexpensive materials that you probably already have at home. Making a wreath for a front door, cute sock bunnies to sit on a mantel or decorating an Easter tree are some of the ways to bring the joy of this season into our homes.

Easter just wouldn't be the same without the activities. The egg hunt is a tradition that goes back hundreds of years, but there are plenty of other ways to keep the whole family busy over the Easter period. The bonnet parade has always been a favourite of mine. I just love seeing the personality and creativity that goes into the elaborate decorated hats. And there's nothing like spending an afternoon on a nature scavenger hunt to remind you of the magic of the season.

My hope is that this book gives you a wealth of inspiration for your Easter celebrations. Within these pages, you will find easy and inexpensive ways to start new traditions that will live on for generations and allow you to make the most wonderful memories for all the family to treasure.

Recipes

Sweet

Savoury

Recipes

Like many families, our Easter holiday celebrations pivot around the kitchen. Meal times are given more gravitas, guests are treated to platters and baked goods, and there are always containers full of homemade treats to dip into. The kitchen is the epicentre of the festivities. It's chaotic, it's messy, but it's very, very fun.

Baking at Easter is a whole-family affair. No matter the age, children can get involved mixing, cutting and decorating baked goods. Many of the recipes in this book are ideal for creating together, and even the smallest helpers can join in. They will love dipping the soft marshmallows into colourful sprinkles to make ears for the Easter cupcakes, or helping to wind the bunny cheese twists into delicious, moreish snacks. Cookie cutters are perfect for younger children and can be used to make cookies, pastry bites and even some craft projects. There's so much joy in the fun shapes that come with Easter. Eggs, bunnies, birds, flowers and even carrots can make the cutest treats.

Of course, there are plenty of sweet foods in our favourite Easter shapes, but savoury items can also be creative and fun. The Spinach and egg potato rosti nests and stuffed pastry carrot cones make lunches that are a treat for the eyes as well as the stomach. I've provided recipes to ensure your Sunday roast is covered whether you are catering for vegans, meat eaters or anyone in between. From the perfect roast chicken to a surprising Vegan Wellington, your guests will happily be tucking into seconds every time.

Sweet

Sweet

Chocolate eggs

Instead of stocking up on basic eggs, why not make Easter feel more special by making your own? It's true that you can walk into any supermarket and buy yourself an egg that would do the job, no matter your budget or dietary needs, but where's the fun in that? Instead of spending the whole day eating chocolate eggs, why not spend some of that time making them? It is just as exciting, far more creative and saves on all the excess packaging that comes with your prepackaged chocolate egg.

Egg moulds are inexpensive and reusable. I use mine year after year with my favourite chocolates. To make your eggs extra special just brush, splatter or drizzle melted chocolate or candy melts into the mould and leave to cool before adding the chocolate. Alternatively, create a marbled effect by swirling white and dark chocolate in the mould and leaving to cool.

Makes 1 large chocolate egg

250g milk chocolate
100g white chocolate or candy
  melts (optional)
100g dark chocolate (optional)

Materials

Egg mould
A sheet or tablecloth
Tissue paper

• •

Here are a few tips before we get started:

- Heat the chocolate in Pyrex bowls set over a pan of simmering water, making sure the base of the bowl does not touch the water.

- Take your time melting the chocolate on a low heat. Once it's almost all melted, remove it from the heat to avoid overheating and turning your silky smooth chocolate into a sticky, lumpy mess.

- Once it's melted, the chocolate will stay liquid for about half an hour (depending on the temperature of your room), but if it does start to harden you can always pop it on the heat again. White chocolate won't reheat well, so melt smaller amounts and try to use it quickly.

- If you're making eggs with little ones, transfer the chocolate into smaller pots to make it easier and safer to use. Always make sure the chocolate is not too hot for small hands.

- Definitely put down a sheet or tablecloth. This gets messy. Some baby wipes are useful to have on hand as well.

See recipe on p. 20 →

Sweet

1. Take the egg mould and spoon in melted chocolate, tipping the mould as you go until you've evenly covered the inside.

2. Turn the mould onto a baking sheet lined with baking paper so it is face down on the flat side. Put this into the freezer for 15 minutes.

3. Repeat these steps 2–3 times until the shell of the egg is thick enough to pop out of the mould.

4. Once the chocolate has set, carefully pull the sides of the mould to let the air in between the mould and the chocolate. Gently press out the chocolate shell from the mould.

5. When you have two halves, spread a little melted chocolate around the flat edges of each half, bring the two halves together and hold in place to secure. Leave them to set and your egg is done. Wrap your egg in tissue paper and store in a cool, dry place.

Tip

If you don't have much time to make your own egg from scratch, you can use a store-bought egg and melt some chocolate to attach candy melts or use it to drizzle and splatter over the egg to make it your own. This is a great way to get very little ones involved.

Flower orange and lemon curd tarts

Continued $\longrightarrow$

Makes 12 tarts

Tarts

1 packet of ready-rolled
   shortcrust pastry
1 jar each of homemade lemon
   and orange curd

Materials

Large flower cookie cutter
   (minimum 8cm wide)
12-hole fairy cake tray x 2

One of my favourite memories of my grandma is making lemon curd tarts together. Her homemade lemon curd tasted like pure heaven and I would not-so-sneakily dip my finger in the curd-filled jam jars for a sweet, zesty treat while we were baking. Like so many women of her generation she cooked using years of practice and intuition, and unfortunately I never did get the recipe from her. But when I taste this fresh lemon curd I'm immediately transported back to days baking in her kitchen.

When I make lemon curd tarts at Easter I get out my flower cutters and it never fails to delight my children. This springtime take on the childhood classic is so very visually pleasing, and using both lemon and orange curd fills the tarts with vibrant colour. Orange curd is just as easy as lemon curd to whip up and makes a refreshing change! I add a tiny drop of orange food colouring to my orange curd to make the colour pop, but this is optional.

Orange or lemon curd

1. Place the orange or lemon zest and juice in in a large pan with the sugar and warm on a low heat until the sugar has dissolved.

2. Add the butter to the pan and stir until melted.

3. Whisk the eggs in a bowl and add to the pan. Stir continuously for 10 minutes or until the mixture is thickened.

4. If you'd like to give your orange curd a more vivid colour, add a drop of orange food colouring and mix well.

Orange curd

Zest and juice of 1 orange
100g sugar
60g butter
2 eggs
Orange food colouring (optional)

Lemon curd

Zest and juice of 2 lemons
100g sugar
60g butter
2 eggs

• •

Tarts

1. Preheat the oven to 200°C/180°C fan/400°F/gas 6.

2. Take the pastry out of the fridge and leave to come up to room temperature for 10 minutes. Roll out on the paper provided.

3. Using a large flower cookie cutter, cut out 12 flowers from the pastry.

4. Grease two shallow fairy cake trays and add the flowers, pressing them down into the spaces. I use two trays because I've found it's easier to miss every other dip in the tray so the pastry flowers have space around them.

1 packet of ready-rolled shortcrust pastry
1 jar each of homemade lemon and orange curd

5. Add a tablespoon of curd to each pastry flower and bake for 10–12 minutes. Remove the tarts from the oven and leave to cool on a wire rack.

Sweet bunny pastries

I think anything tastes better if it comes in a sweet bunny-shaped package. It also helps if it's full of fresh strawberries and whipped cream! These are an irresistible treat with a cup of tea and make a delightfully light Easter dessert. The strawberries add a fresh sweetness that is delicious on a warm spring day, especially if the sun is out. They can be whipped up in around 15 minutes, so they are perfect if you need something in a pinch, but also great for baking with younger children who might not have the longest attention span.

I've used a large rabbit-shaped cookie cutter to make the pastry shapes. You could also easily cut a rabbit head and ears, egg or rough flower shapes with a knife if you don't have any Easter-themed cutters to hand. If you're making these with children you could ask them to draw a simple shape on a piece of card, then cut this out and use it as a template to cut your pastry. Their art will then become an edible treat right in front of their eyes!

Makes 12

1 packet of ready-rolled puff pastry
200ml double cream
50g sugar
1 tsp vanilla extract
200g strawberries, sliced
Icing sugar, for dusting

Materials

Large rabbit cookie cutter

1. Preheat the oven to 200°C/180°C fan/400°F/gas 6.

2. Take the pastry out of the fridge and leave to come up to room temperature for 10 minutes. Roll out on the paper provided.

3. Using a rabbit cookie cutter, cut out 12 rabbit shapes and place them onto a lined baking tray. Bake for 10–15 minutes and leave to cool on a wire rack.

4. Whip the cream, sugar and vanilla extract in a bowl using a hand blender for 5 minutes until it has thickened.

5. Cut each rabbit pastry in half to make two rabbit shapes. Pipe the cream into the middle of the two sides and add the sliced strawberries.

6. Place one half of the rabbit back onto the other to create a very sweet rabbit sandwich. Dust a little icing sugar onto each and serve.

Meringue nests

Makes 8

1 tbsp vinegar
3 egg whites
150g sugar
Blue, red, yellow and
    green gel food colouring
200g double cream
50g icing sugar, plus extra
    for dusting
80g chocolate mini eggs
    (I used Cadbury Mini Eggs)

Materials

Toothpick
Piping bags
Large nozzles
Rolling pin

Everything looks more fun in pastel colours. These meringue nests are a classic spring treat given a colourful makeover. I've separated my meringue mix into four and added a tiny amount of food colouring to each section before adding them to the piping bags. You could skip this step and make your nests all the same colour if you prefer, but I love this pastel aesthetic and it's worth a few extra minutes work in my view.

The size of the nests is in your control. You can scale down the nests to make smaller portion sizes for younger children, or even serve them as bite-sized nibbles for a dessert table. Just ensure that if children are eating these nests the mini eggs have been broken up into very small pieces or even chocolate dust to avoid choking hazards.

See recipe on p. 28 $\longrightarrow$

1. Preheat the oven to 120°C/100°C fan/250°F/gas 1 or as low as your oven will go.

2. In a large, very clean mixing bowl or free-standing mixer, add the vinegar and egg whites. Whisk on a high power with an electric mixer for 4–5 minutes.

3. Start adding the sugar a little at a time. Continue to whisk as you add the sugar for another 3–4 minutes until you have stiff peaks.

4. Divide the mixture into four bowls and add a small amount of food colouring using a toothpick. Whisk the food colouring into each meringue mixture and spoon into separate piping bags with a large nozzle.

5. Pipe a round base of meringue onto a sheet of baking paper, starting in the middle and spiralling out. When your base is roughly 10cm in diameter, pipe the wall of the nest over the outer ring of the base.

6. Bake in the oven for 1 hour 45 minutes. Once the meringue nests have finished cooking, keep in a closed oven for as long as possible. Ideally overnight.

7. To make the filling, whip the double cream and icing sugar together for around 2 minutes until thick. Spoon the cream into the cooled nests. Crush the chocolate mini eggs with a rolling pin. Sprinkle over the nests with a dusting of icing sugar and serve.

Making meringues is actually quite easy, here are some tips to ensure a crisp exterior and light, chewy interior

- Ensure your bowl is very clean. I always clean and dry mine thoroughly right before making meringue.

- Before adding the eggs, add a teaspoon of vinegar for each egg to the bowl.

- I always use my trusty hand blender but if you have a stand mixer this will work as well. If you really want a workout you can whip by hand, but it can take up to 20 minutes, so it's no easy task.

- Make sure you whip until you have those stiff peaks.

Easter Swiss roll

Continued →

Makes 8 servings

40g self-raising flour
1 tsp cornflour
1 egg
30g caster sugar
20g softened butter
Green and yellow gel food colouring

Sponge

3 eggs
1 tsp white vinegar
75g caster sugar
75g self-raising flour
1 tbsp cornflour
1 tsp vanilla extract
Icing sugar, for dusting

Filling

3 tbsp lemon curd
300ml double cream
50g icing sugar
Zest of 1 lemon

Materials

Piping bags with small nozzle
(optional)
Silicone Swiss roll mat or Swiss
roll tin

I have a real soft spot for the humble Swiss roll. As cakes go, this one deserves a place on every table for every and any occasion. In fact, I could write a whole book on creating variations on this classic cake. It's just so versatile and always looks and tastes amazing. It's a cake you can easily tailor to your own skill level and there are also so many ways of changing the flavour, style and finished look of this cake to suit the celebration.

I love a simple fresh lemon cake, so I've decided our Easter Swiss roll will be a celebration of citrus. It's a light, pleasingly sweet end to any meal, especially in warmer weather. These patterned roll cakes are a Japanese invention that look stunning but you would not believe how incredibly easy they are to create. The pattern is made by piping out your design onto the baking paper using a thicker cake batter. After freezing you then pour the cake mixture over the design and bake. You can alter the design batter to create patterns, pictures and colours in a way that is much easier than using traditional icing decorations.

Sweet

1. To make the design batter, sift the flour into a bowl or free-standing mixer, and add the cornflour. Mix well before adding the egg white (reserving the yolk for the sponge), sugar, vanilla extract and softened butter. Whisk into a thick batter.

2. Spoon a third of the mixture into a separate bowl. Add the green food colouring to the smaller bowl and the yellow food colouring to the larger portion and mix well. Then add to piping bags. Either use a small nozzle or cut a very small hole at the end of the piping bag.

3. Grease a silicone Swiss roll mat or a Swiss roll tin lined with baking paper (add extra grease to the baking paper to help stop the cake splitting).

4. Pipe the outline of each lemon with the yellow batter. Once the entire surface is covered in lemon outlines, make the hole bigger and fill each one in. Using the green batter, make a little leaf at the top of each lemon. Place the tray into the freezer to set for about an hour.

5. Preheat the oven to 200°C/180°C fan/400°F/gas 6. To make the sponge batter, take two large bowls and split the egg whites into one bowl and the yolks into the other. Add the vinegar to the egg whites then pour in half of the sugar. Add the extra yolk left over from the design batter to the yolk bowl then pour in the remaining sugar.

6. Whisk the egg whites using an electric hand whisk or mixer for about 4 minutes until you have soft peaks. Then whisk the egg yolks for 1–2 minutes until light and frothy. Add the egg whites to the yolk mixture and gently fold together.

7. Sift the flour into a bowl and add the cornflour. Mix well, then add this to the egg mixture and gently fold together. Spread the mixture evenly over the lemon shapes and bake for 8–10 minutes until the sponge is springy and is starting to brown.

8. Remove from the oven and, if using a silicone mat, place onto a wire rack or baking tray. Place a clean tea towel and then a baking tray on top. Carefully flip upside down and gently peel off the baking paper or silicone mat to reveal the design. Lay a second tea towel over the top and using another baking tray, flip the cake again. Dust this side of the cake with icing sugar, cover again with the tea towel and roll into the Swiss roll shape. Leave to cool for an hour.

9. Once the cake is cool, unroll it. Cut the edges straight and spread a layer of lemon curd onto the non-design side. Whip the cream, icing sugar and lemon zest until thick then spread this over the curd. Roll the sponge again and serve.

Tip

I made my green food colouring by mixing together blue and yellow. If you do this, take care to only use a tiny amount of blue food colouring. I use a toothpick to be more exact with the amounts.

Simnel cake

175g softened butter
175g sugar
3 eggs
225g plain flour
1 tsp baking powder
½ tsp ground ginger
½ tsp ground cinnamon
25g ground almonds
100g glace cherries
50g crystallised ginger
500g mixed fruit
Icing sugar, for dusting
500g marzipan
2 tbsp apricot jam

Materials

20cm round cake tin

This is a cake for all you marzipan lovers. I am partial to a piece of marzipan or two but it seems to divide opinion. Here it is a wonderfully nutty addition to this classic fruit cake. The eleven marzipan balls adorning the top of the cake traditionally represent Jesus's disciples. All except for Judas, who for obvious reasons does not get a place on the cake.

My absolute favourite marzipan to use with this recipe is clementine marzipan. This is usually only available in shops over Christmas, so if you're really organised add an extra block of this to your store cupboard for the Easter season. If not, it's completely fine to use normal marzipan, or you can even make your own if you have a recipe you enjoy.

The cake itself is a much lighter version of a Christmas cake. Still full of delicious fruits and spices but without the need to store and feed the cake for weeks before icing. The texture is more spongy and is not as heavily fruited. Everyone will want a slice or two for an afternoon tea treat.

Continued →

Sweet

33

1. Preheat the oven to 170°C/150°C fan/350°F/gas 4. Grease and line a 20cm cake tin with baking paper.

2. In a large bowl or free-standing mixer, cream together the butter and sugar. Add the eggs one at a time and gently mix into the butter mixture. Once combined, whisk for another minute until light and fluffy.

3. Sift the flour into a separate bowl. Add the baking powder, ground ginger, cinnamon and almonds and mix well. Add the flour mixture to the butter, sugar and eggs and mix until combined.

4. Chop the cherries and crystallised ginger and add them to the batter along with the mixed fruit.

5. Pour the batter into the cake tin and bake. After 1 hour and 30 minutes cover the cake tin with foil and bake for another 20–30 minutes. Check the cake is ready by sticking a metal skewer or knife into the cake. Once this comes out clean the cake is ready.

6. Dust your work surface with icing sugar and roll out the marzipan to the thickness of a pound coin. Using the cake tin as a template, cut out a circle of marzipan. Heat the jam in a pan with a teaspoon of water. Brush the jam over the top of the cake and lay the marzipan on top. Crimp the edges using your thumb and finger on one hand and one finger on the other. Roll the rest of the marzipan into 11 balls, then dab each one with a little jam on the bottom before placing it onto the cake. Dust with icing sugar and serve.

Vegan rabbit sugar cookies

My husband has been vegan for many years now and in that time vegan options have become more and more popular. These days it's easy to find a dairy-free Easter egg, but I remember years ago making one because the health food shop close to us had sold out. But even though it's much easier to find vegan alternatives these days, I still love to keep with our tradition and make something special just for him every year.

These vegan sugar cookies are made from a recipe I've used for years. It's never failed me and it tastes amazing. I recently started making vegan royal icing and it's cheaper and just as easy to whip up as when you're making it with eggs. I actually prefer it now! And what better way to celebrate our vegan loved ones than with the cutest vegans you'll ever meet: these sweet little rabbit cookies!

Piping royal icing takes a little bit of practice but you soon get the hang of it. The most important thing is getting the consistency of the icing just right. Your firmer icing should stay in place as you pipe the edges of your design. The softer icing is to fill in the areas you have created with it, and it should spread easily over the surface of the cookie. You can use a toothpick to help push it right to the edges. If it's too thick add a little lemon juice. If it's too thin add a teaspoon of icing sugar and mix.

Makes 50 cookies

190g icing sugar
230g vegan margarine
60ml almond milk
600g plain flour, plus extra
  for dusting
2 tbsp cornflour
1 tsp baking soda
1 tsp cream of tartar
1 tsp vanilla extract

Materials

Rabbit head cookie cutter

1. In a bowl or free-standing mixer, beat the icing sugar into the margarine and almond milk. Once whipped, stir in the flour, cornflour, baking soda, cream of tartar and vanilla. Cover the bowl and leave in the fridge for at least an hour.

2. Preheat your oven to 200°C/180°C fan/400°F/gas 6. Lay out a baking sheet and sprinkle flour over it. Spoon out a quarter of your mixture and sprinkle flour over the top. Knead gently until it's firm. Sprinkle again with flour and roll out until the dough is around 5mm thick.

3. Cut out the rabbit heads with a cookie cutter and transfer to a lined baking tray. Bake for 8–10 minutes until the edges begin to brown. Transfer to a cooling rack.

Continued ⟶

Vegan royal icing

60ml aquafaba
  (the liquid from
  a can of chickpeas)
5 tsp lemon juice
  or white vinegar
700g icing sugar
1 tsp vanilla extract
Red, brown and black gel
  food colouring
Black ready to roll icing

Materials

Piping bags

1. In a bowl or free-standing mixer, whisk together the aquafaba and lemon juice or vinegar until frothy. Add the icing sugar and whisk on a medium speed for around 8 minutes until the consistency is smooth and thick.

2. Split the icing into four bowls and add a little gel food colouring to three of the bowls. Spoon half of each mixture into individual piping bags (this will be for lining).

3. Add a teaspoon of lemon juice to the remaining icing in each bowl. Mix well and add more lemon juice if needed. You want a thick but runny consistency, then add this to four more piping bags.

4. Snip off a small hole at the ends of the first piping bags and draw your details onto the rabbit. Cut a slightly larger hole in the second set of piping bags and fill these areas.

5. Once you've added the colour to the rabbits, leave the icing to dry. When hardened, you can add the eye and mouth details with the firmer black icing from step 3, or by using black ready to roll icing.

Easter cupcakes

Makes 12 cupcakes

175g butter
175g caster sugar
3 large eggs
175g self-raising flour
1 tsp baking powder
1 tsp vanilla extract

Topping

150g butter
300g icing sugar
Pink gel food colouring
12 large marshmallows
Sprinkles

Materials

12 cupcake cases
12-hole cupcake tray
Piping bag
Large nozzle

My favourite kind of baking is a simple, easy and quick recipe that has a big visual impact, and tastes great as well, of course. No party is complete without a cupcake and they are always the first to go at our get-togethers. My children think these are the most incredible cakes on Earth and I definitely get mum points when I make them. Just don't tell them how easy they are to make quite yet!

What makes these cupcakes so easy are the bunny ears. This very simple technique is perfect for anyone who isn't confident or hasn't had a lot of experience with piped icing. They steal the show and it takes just seconds to turn your cupcakes from a blob of icing into adorable little bunnies. If your icing is a little messy they do a great job of hiding any lumps and bumps, making your cupcakes look flawless as well as super fun. Adding sprinkles to the marshmallow ears is just the next level of cuteness. You can use sprinkles in different shapes and colours to give each bunny its own personality.

Continued $\longrightarrow$

1. Preheat the oven to 190°C/170°C fan/375°F/gas 5.

2. Add the butter and sugar to a large mixing bowl or free-standing mixer, and whisk until light and creamy. Add the eggs and continue to whisk until combined.

3. Sift the flour into the bowl and add the baking powder and vanilla extract. Whisk on a low speed until combined.

4. Place 12 cupcake cases into a cupcake tray and divide the batter evenly among them. Bake in the oven for 15 minutes. Test that the cakes are cooked by pushing a sharp knife into a cake. If the knife comes out clean, your cakes are ready. If not, bake for a few more minutes before testing again. Leave to cool on a wire rack.

5. To make the icing, combine the butter and icing sugar in a bowl. Whisk on a low speed for around 4 minutes until light and fluffy. Add a drop of pink food colouring and mix well into the icing. Add a little more if needed until you have the desired colour.

6. Add the icing to a piping bag fitted with a large nozzle. Slowly pipe the icing onto the cupcakes in circles to create a swirled effect.

7. To make the ears, cut the marshmallows diagonally from flat side to flat side using a sharp knife. Dip the sticky cut section into the sprinkles and place two onto each cupcake to create the ears.

Hot cross bun bread and butter pudding

The minute the hot cross buns start stacking up in the supermarket I'm there, ready to fill my basket. I look forward to this moment from the minute Christmas is over and I cannot resist a hot cross bun with my afternoon tea, toasted and covered in butter. But I've found an even more delicious way of serving hot cross buns that combine two of my favourite sweet bread treats. This hot cross bun bread and butter pudding is a warm, comforting, delicious fusion that is guaranteed not to disappoint.

The best thing about bread and butter pudding is its versatility. You can pretty much throw anything into the mixture and it will just work. I love adding some extra dried fruits or even crystallised ginger if I'm feeling like something fiery. For this recipe I've added orange zest for a refreshing hint of citrus. Serve your bread and butter pudding with cream, or if the sun is shining a scoop of vanilla ice cream and you'll be in heaven!

Makes 6 servings

6 hot cross buns
Butter, for spreading
150ml milk
150ml cream
3 eggs
40g sugar
1 tsp vanilla extract
Zest of 1 orange

Materials

20cm x 25cm roasting tray

• •

1. Preheat the oven to 190°C/170°C fan/375°F/gas 5.

2. Split up your hot cross buns and cut them in half. Butter the insides of the buns and put them back together. Add the buns to the roasting tray.

3. In a bowl or free-standing mixer, whisk the milk, cream, eggs, sugar, vanilla extract and orange zest together until smooth. Pour over the buns in the tray.

4. Bake in the oven for 30–35 minutes until the mixture is light and puffs up. The pudding should be spongy to touch. Remove from the oven and leave to cool for 5 minutes before serving.

See image on p.42 →

Sweet

Easter egg cheesecake

Makes 6 small individual cheesecakes or 2 large individual cheesecakes

40g unsalted butter
100g digestive biscuits
6 small chocolate egg halves
400g full-fat soft cheese
100g thick double cream
100g caster sugar
Juice of ½ lemon
Orange and yellow gel
  food colouring
80g chocolate mini eggs
Grated white chocolate

Materials

3 piping bags
Serrated nozzle

Since having children Easter has definitely become more about the chocolate. I love that our families get excited about buying chocolate Easter eggs for our two little ones, but they might sometimes go a little overboard and we often end up with far too many, even for me to eat... just don't tell my children that! This is a way to take all those extra eggs and do something a little different with them.

If you don't have an abundance of chocolate eggs you can still enjoy an Easter egg cheesecake! You can either buy the eggs to make these or you can make your own (see page 19). Most Easter eggs are made using a standard milk chocolate, but I've used a lemon drizzle white chocolate in a small egg mould to create these indulgent no-bake lemon cheesecakes. The bright, zesty flavour gives this cheesecake a light but indulgent taste that will leave you wanting more. If I was making these with a milk chocolate egg I would substitute the lemon juice for a teaspoon of vanilla extract.

Continued —>

1. Melt the butter in a pan. Blend the biscuits to a fine crumb and add them to the melted butter. Mix together until all of the biscuit crumb is buttery. Leave to fully cool then spoon roughly 2 tablespoons into each chocolate egg half until the base of the egg is covered. Gently press it down using the back of a spoon to create a flat, even surface. Chill in the fridge while making the topping.

2. Put the soft cheese, double cream, sugar and lemon juice into a bowl and use a mixer to combine. When the mixture is thick and light, spoon it into the chocolate eggs until level with the sides.

3. Place the remaining topping mixture into three bowls and add a tiny amount of gel food colouring to each bowl, leaving one without. Mix well and add to three piping bags with a serrated nozzle in each.

4. Hover your icing bag over the filled egg half and gently squeeze until the filling comes out. Make a small ball of filling and pull the piping bag up as you stop squeezing. Repeat over the top of the egg half using all three colours to cover. Add a few mini eggs and a sprinkle of grated chocolate to the top and chill in the fridge for a couple of hours before serving.

Carrot cake truffles

Makes 30 truffles

150ml vegetable oil
3 eggs
200g caster sugar
200g carrots
200g self-raising flour
1 tsp baking powder
½ tsp mixed spice
½ tsp ground cinnamon
½ tsp ground ginger
150g full fat soft cheese
100g white chocolate
100g crushed walnuts or grated
  chocolate, to decorate

Materials

24cm round cake tin
Pyrex bowl
Skewer or corn-on-the-cob holder

If you're looking to make your Easter Sunday meal feel really special, think about going small. One of my favourite ways to make a meal feel like more of an event is to serve a range of desserts, but after a Sunday roast even just one dessert can often feel more like a chore than a treat. My solution is to make everything smaller. Instead of having to decide on just the one thing, your guests can choose bite-sized bits of everything on offer. It's such a wonderfully indulgent way to serve your classic cakes and desserts. Imagine a tiered cake stand covered in small bites for your guests to choose from and enjoy. It's the ultimate way to cater for everyone's tastes.

Alternatively these are lovely to have on a plate as an afternoon sweet nibble. These carrot cake truffles are so deliciously moreish your guests won't be able to resist. I can never eat just one. Carrot cake is an all-time favourite for me. This moist, spicy cake which is full of flavour works so well as a truffle. It's also a fantastic way to use up any leftover, dry cake as we add additional cream cheese to this mixture to make the cake even more soft and squidgy.

See recipe on p.48 ⟶

1. Preheat the oven to 180°C/160°C fan/350°F/gas 4.

2. Combine the vegetable oil, eggs and sugar in a bowl. Grate the carrot into a separate bowl with the flour, baking powder and spices. Mix well then add the wet ingredients to the dry. Stir together until all the flour is coated in the wet ingredients.

3. Grease and line a 24cm cake tin with baking paper. Pour the cake mixture into the tin and bake for 35–40 minutes. Check that the cake is cooked by inserting a clean knife it. If it comes out clean, then your cake is ready to take out of the oven. Leave to cool for 10 minutes.

4. Crumble the cake into a large bowl and add the soft cheese. Mix well until it is all the same consistency. Scoop out a heaped tablespoon and roll into a ball in your hands. Place onto a lined baking tray. Repeat for the remaining mixture and place the baking tray in the freezer for an hour.

5. Melt the white chocolate in a Pyrex bowl over a pan of water. Keeping the heat on low, remove the cake truffles from the freezer. Push a skewer or corn on the cob holder into the truffle and dip into the chocolate. Allow the excess to drip from the truffle and place back onto the lined baking tray. Repeat with the remaining cake truffles. Before the chocolate sets you can add a topping of crushed walnuts or grated chocolate. Cool and serve.

Savoury

Savoury

Stuffed pastry carrot cones

When there are so many creative sweet foods on offer sometimes it's hard for the savoury items to feel as appealing. But these soft, cheese-filled pastry carrot cones tick all the boxes. This mock carrot snack will have your little bunnies nibbling away in no time! They are delicious served as a snack or with a side of salad for a very fun lunch.

You don't need any special kitchen equipment to make these. I shaped my carrots around ice cream cones. And the best part is the ice cream cones can still be eaten after baking. No waste at all! Just cut a piece of kitchen foil about 10cm long and cut this in half along the width to make two pieces. Wrap these diagonally around the straight conical section of the ice cream cone and they're ready to use.

A trick I like to use to make the pastry more orange is using just the yolk as an egg wash. As this browns the pastry, it turns a slightly orange hue, which finishes the carrot cones perfectly.

Makes 8 cones

1 packet of ready-rolled puff pastry
1 egg yolk, beaten
300g full-fat soft cheese
1 tbsp milk
Large bunch of parsley
1 tsp minced garlic
Salt and pepper

Materials

8 ice cream cones
Kitchen foil
Piping bag

• •

1. Preheat the oven to 200°C/180°C fan/400°F/gas 6.

2. Wrap the outside of eight ice-cream cones in kitchen foil. Roll out the pastry and cut into long strips 2.5cm wide.

3. Starting at the smallest end of the cone, wrap the pastry from one end to the other, slightly overlapping to create a pastry cone. Brush the pastry with the egg yolk.

4. Bake for 12–15 minutes. Remove from the oven and leave to cool slightly before gently pulling the ice-cream cone and foil from the inside of the pastry cone. This is easier to do when the cone is warm, but as the pastry is still soft and very delicate, you will need to take care not to crush the cone.

5. In a large bowl or free-standing mixer, whip the soft cheese and milk together on a high speed for 2–3 minutes until it is light and fluffy. Chop half of the parsley. Add the parsley and the garlic to the whipped cheese and stir in well. Season with salt and pepper to taste. Spoon the mixture into a piping bag and cut off the end.

6. Squeeze the soft cheese mixture into the centre of the cones until they are filled. Then add a few sprigs of the remaining parsley to the cream cheese to look like carrot tops.

Bunny cheese twists

This twist on a party classic is a real crowd pleaser. A cheese twist is always popular, but make it into a bunny for Easter and it's gold. They can be whipped up at a moment's notice and stored for a few days in an airtight container for quick Easter-themed snacks.

We make these as a family with two young children, and while half the cheese might not always make it into the twists, baking these bunnies is such a fun half an hour in the kitchen. They are so simple to make that my two-year-old can try most of the steps and they both love to help me twist the pastry and pinch the ears into shape, almost as much as they love to help me eat them!

Makes 12-16 twists

2 packets of ready-rolled puff pastry
Flour, for dusting
100g mature Cheddar
20g hard cheese
1 egg

Materials

Rolling pin

● ●

1. Preheat the oven to 200°C/180°C fan/400°F/gas 6.

2. Sprinkle flour onto a clean dry surface and lay out a ready-rolled sheet of puff pastry. Grate both the Cheddar and hard cheese and sprinkle evenly over the surface of the pastry.

3. Lay the second sheet of pastry over the top of the first and gently press down by running a rolling pin over the top. Take a fork and press it into the pastry along the two shortest edges to seal the pastry together.

4. Cut the combined sheets of pastry into strips 1.5cm wide, running parallel to the longest side. Then twist the pastry strips and gently fold in half. Wrap the two ends together around the middle and place onto an oven tray lined with baking paper. Shape the pastry so there's a circle at the folded end and the ends of the pastry are pinched to a point and shaped like ears.

5. Beat the egg and brush over the top of the pastry twists. Bake in the oven for 12–15 minutes until the pastry is a golden colour.

Spring garden focaccia

Easily the best thing about spring is all the colour. The explosion of green that almost comes out of nowhere after months of grey. The crocuses, bluebells and daffodils that blanket the ground create such a joyful moment. I love to mirror this hopeful, springtime vibrancy in the kitchen when I'm baking. This beautiful focaccia bread is a stunning way to celebrate at meal times these magical changes that are happening in nature.

But this bread is not only beautiful. Focaccia is outrageously delicious and all the extra ingredients add a different flavour with each mouthful. It's so enticingly moreish, I can't help but tear off pieces throughout the day to snack on.

This is also a great way of using up any leftovers in your fridge. I like to whip this up at the end of the week with whatever is left, which makes my focaccia different every time. Creating the patterns and floral forms on top of the bread is such an enjoyable and low-pressure creative outlet. The bread will be eaten however your art turns out, so let go of the idea that it needs to be perfect. Have fun and experiment with your veggie creation.

Makes 8 servings

7g yeast
400ml lukewarm water
500g strong bread flour
2 tsp salt
5 tbsp olive oil
Butter, for greasing
Small amounts of tomatoes, peppers, red onion, garlic, basil and flat-leaf parsley

Materials

Shallow medium-sized oven dish

• •

Continued →

Savoury

1. Put the yeast into a small bowl and pour the water over it. Quickly whisk and leave for 5 minutes for the yeast to activate.

2. In a separate bowl mix together the flour and salt. Make a well in the middle and pour in the water and yeast. Using a rubber spatula mix the flour and water together until no dry flour is left.

3. In a bowl at least twice the size of the dough, pour 3 tablespoons of the oil, then scrape the dough over the top of the oil. Turn the dough over in the oil making sure it is coated, then cover the bowl with cling film or a lid and leave in the fridge for between 10–24 hours until the dough has doubled in size.

4. Grease a shallow oven dish with butter, then add the remaining tablespoons of oil. Place the dough over the oil and pull it out to the corners of the dish with your fingers.

5. Thinly slice your vegetables and place them and the herbs onto the dough to create the garden design. Cover the dish with cling film and leave for another 4 hours to rise.

6. Preheat the oven to 220°C/200°C fan/425°F/gas 7. Bake for 20–30 minutes depending on the size of the pan. For a larger pan with a thinner dough, cook for a shorter time. If you're using a smaller pan and making a thicker dough, bake for longer.

Tip

Get creative with your toppings! Spring onions, sun-dried tomatoes, olives, edible flowers, courgette and artichoke all work well to create a tasty Easter dish.

Roast chicken

Is there any meal better to share with family than a roast? As traditions go this one brings generations to the table all to enjoy the same comforting, time-honoured meal. You can't go wrong with a classic roast chicken cooked well. It is the ultimate crowd pleaser. Juicy on the inside, with a crispy, flavourful skin, whatever your guests' preference is, this chicken is there for all to enjoy.

Another reason a roast chicken works so well at Easter is the weather. It is such a versatile meat that can be served in limitless ways depending on the time of day, the season or occasion. Roast chicken can be served with Hasselback potatoes (see page 66) and salad for a bright and warm spring day lunch, or on colder days add homemade gravy and mash for a hearty and comforting meal that will leave everyone feeling warm and content.

The trick to getting your roast chicken just right is basting. You want to cover the skin in those delicious juices from the bottom of the pan at least once during the cooking process. Smaller chickens (1–1.2kg) will need at least 1 hour 20 minutes and large chickens (1.8–2kg) at least 1 hour 40 minutes. After this time check the juices run clear from the meat in several places. I also cut into the meat to check there are no parts that are pink and undercooked just to be extra careful.

Small chicken serves 2-4, large chicken serves 4-6

2 tbsp olive oil

3 carrots

2 onions

1 bulb of garlic

1 whole chicken

1 lemon

A few sprigs of fresh rosemary and thyme

Salt

1 tbsp flour

250ml chicken stock

Materials

Roasting tin (large enough to comfortably fit the chicken)

Kitchen foil

Continued →

Savoury

59

1. Preheat the oven to 200°C/180°C fan/400°F/gas 6. Add 1 tablespoon of the olive oil to a large roasting tin. Roughly chop the carrots and onions into large pieces. Break open the bulb of garlic and gently crush the individual cloves to release the flavour. Place the vegetables and garlic into the roasting tin and stir to mix.

2. Place your chicken on top of the vegetables. Cut the lemon in half and insert into the chicken along with the fresh herbs. Rub the remaining oil onto the chicken skin and season with salt.

3. Cook the chicken for 45 minutes, then remove from the oven and spoon the juices from the bottom of the tin over the chicken. Cook for another 35 minutes. Remove from the oven and check that the chicken is cooked through. If the chicken needs more time in the oven, baste in the juices again and cook for an additional 10 minutes. Check again and cook for longer if needed. Once the chicken is cooked, transfer it to a board and cover with kitchen foil to rest for 20 minutes.

4. To make gravy, strain the chicken juices into a pan over a low heat and add 1 tablespoon of flour. Stir into a paste, then add the chicken stock. Stir continuously until the gravy is thickened.

Spinach and egg potato rosti nests

My children are not potato lovers. I have no idea where they get it from as I have never met a potato I wouldn't eat every day for the rest of my life. So I've made it my life's mission to find potato recipes that they will happily eat and that we can enjoy together as a family. This rosti nest has a crispier, crunchier texture than most potatoes and adds the fun factor to serving, especially around Easter. They love this recipe, even if I have to adapt the filling to their favourite veggie for that month.

This works well as a simple lunch or as part of a bigger meal with salad or extra greens. It's also really tasty with bacon as an indulgent breakfast. To be honest, I eat this year round, but it's particularly fun to play with the nest theme for an extra-special Easter treat.

Makes 4 nests

1 small red onion
Butter, for frying and greasing
3 large waxy potatoes
A handful of spinach
Salt and pepper
Bacon or avocado
1 egg
Chopped fresh chives
  or oregano

Materials

Large muffin tin

1. Preheat the oven to 180°C/160°C fan/350°F/gas 4.

2. Finely slice the red onion. Melt a knob of butter in a frying pan on a medium heat and caramelise the red onion until brown.

3. Peel and grate the potatoes into a large bowl. Chop the spinach and add to the potato with the caramelised onion. Season with salt and pepper and mix well.

4. Heat a small saucepan over a medium heat. Melt a knob of butter in the pan and add enough of the potato mix to cover the bottom. Cook for 5 minutes then flip over to the other side. Cook for another 5 minutes.

5. Grease a large muffin tin and slide the potato rosti into a muffin cup, pressing down with a spoon to create the shape. Place this in the oven for 10–15 minutes while you make the fillings.

6. Cook your bacon to your liking and poach an egg in boiling water for 4 minutes to get the perfect runny yoke. As your egg is cooking, remove the rosti and let it cool for a few minutes. Spoon it out of the muffin tin and onto a plate. Add the bacon or chopped avocado and egg and sprinkle with chopped chives or oregano and pepper.

Vegan Wellington

Makes 6 servings

500g cooked lentils
1 large onion
2 carrots
150g mushrooms
4 cloves of garlic
3 tbsp oats
1 tsp paprika
1 tbsp soy sauce
2 tbsp nutritional yeast
1 tsp vegan Worcestershire sauce
1 packet of ready-rolled puff pastry
Soya or nut milk
A few flat-leaf parsley leaves

Materials

Loaf tin

I have been making vegan Wellingtons for many years now. Finding meat substitutes or even ready-made freezer food that was more than just a simple vegetable burger was once very difficult. I regularly make a nut roast, but on special occasions I like to bring out the big guns and make a vegan Wellington.

I've made Wellingtons with meat substitutes, whole vegetables and pate and chopped, chunky fillings, but this style is my favourite for a few reasons. For this Wellington, I have blended the filling and baked it to create a loaf to wrap the pastry around. This way it's easy to add your choice of proteins and pack them full of flavour. This works amazingly well with lentils, beans, tofu, nuts, seeds and green leafy vegetables. The trick is frying and then baking to remove as much liquid as possible before assembling.

I've always used shop-bought pastry to make my Wellington. This is almost always vegan, but check the ingredients for milk and dairy products before baking this for that favourite vegan in your life.

1. Preheat the oven to 200°C/180°C fan/400°F/gas 6.

2. Drain the lentils and press the excess water out of them. Chop the onion, carrots, mushrooms and garlic and fry on a medium heat until soft.

3. Add the lentils and vegetables to a blender with the oats, paprika, soy sauce, nutritional yeast and vegan Worcestershire sauce. Pulse together until the ingredients are combined but still have a rough texture.

4. Line a loaf tin with plenty of baking paper to fold over the edges. Fill the tin with your lentil and mushroom mix and press down. Cook for 45 minutes then remove from the oven. Using the extra paper, lift the loaf out of the tin and place onto a baking tray. The loaf should now stay in shape. Place the tray back in the oven and cook for another 45 minutes. Remove from the oven and leave to cool.

5. Unroll the pastry, place the loaf on top and wrap the pastry over, cutting off any excess. Lightly score the top of the pastry and wash with the milk. Bake the Wellington on 200°C/180°C fan/400°F/gas 6 for 15 minutes. Remove from the oven and leave to sit for 10 minutes. Sprinkle with chopped flat-leaf parsley before serving.

Hasselback potatoes

This is one of my favourite ways to serve potatoes. Light and crispy and full of flavour. An elevated mini jacket potato that looks as good as it tastes. Before I made hasselback potatoes myself I always thought they looked a bit of a hassle to make, but there's actually one very simple trick to cutting the slices quickly and easily.

Once you have cleaned and dried your potato, place it onto a chopping board. Take either two chopsticks or two wooden spoon handles and place one on either side of the potato lengthwise. Using a sharp knife, begin to slice into the potato from one end. The knife will stop as it reaches the chopsticks or spoon handles, which leaves a section of potato uncut at the bottom. This technique allows you to quickly cut your slices at the same depth and keeps the potato intact to cook and serve.

All that's left to do is pack your potato full of flavour. I've used a garlic purée for this recipe as I tend to have this on hand for quick dinners. You can also easily mince your garlic in a garlic crusher or using a pestle and mortar to create an oil coating that sets these potatoes apart. Serve this as a delicious, hearty side that goes perfectly with the Vegan Wellington on page 64.

Makes 4–6 servings

10–12 Maris Piper potatoes
A few sprigs of fresh rosemary
  and thyme
3 tbsp olive oil
1 tsp garlic purée or minced garlic
Salt and pepper
Vine cherry tomatoes

Materials

Chopsticks or 2 wooden spoons
20cm x 25cm roasting tin

1. Preheat the oven to 200°C/180°C fan/400°F/gas 6.

2. Thoroughly wash the potatoes in cold water. On a chopping board place the potato between two chopsticks or spoon handles. Thinly slice the potato and place into a small roasting tin. Repeat until the tin is full.

3. Chop the herbs and mix together with the olive oil and garlic in a bowl. Pour over the potatoes. Gently push each one open, allowing the oil to infuse into the potato. Season with salt and pepper and put in the oven for 30 minutes.

4. Remove the tin from the oven and add the tomatoes on the vine. Using a spoon, scoop up the oil from the bottom of the tin and drizzle over both the tomatoes and the potatoes. Put the tin back into the oven for 15–20 minutes or until the potatoes have started to crisp on the outside. Remove from the oven and serve.

Crafts

Decorations

Play

Crafts

If there was a holiday made for crafting with all the family, it has to be Easter. It's that time of year when you can't quite rely on the weather to be fair enough for day-long outdoor activities. Instead having a backup crafting activity ready to whip up from materials you already have in your home can keep boredom at bay.

There's something about the themes of Easter that children love. Simple shapes, cute animals and bright colours pique their interest, and an easy craft activity can turn into an afternoon of creativity and play. I ran out of cereal boxes making more and more of our nature bunny masks over several days and I still get regular requests to make the rainbow salt dough we use to make our colourful ornaments. My younger children love these projects but I've also included crafts that are for older children or that you might like to do alone – slower projects that give you a moment to breathe in the changing world around you and feel connected to nature.

Many of our Easter craft projects take inspiration from nature, but in some I've used elements of the world around us to create something beautiful. Dyeing eggs with natural dyes is something anyone can do at home to make organic, earthy colours. I have also harnessed the beauty of the natural world by using seeds and dried beans to make mosaic ornaments in stunning, muted colours. Most of the projects in this book use natural or recycled materials. When the weather permits, it's a wonderful time of year to get outside and forage for your crafting supplies! We take baskets and look for interesting weeds, fallen petals and leaves that we can use to craft with. It's such a wonderful way to feel connected to the changing seasons and experience the world waking up all around us.

Decorations

Decorations

Gelatine egg sun-catchers

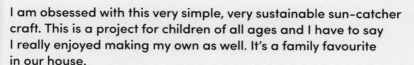

I am obsessed with this very simple, very sustainable sun-catcher craft. This is a project for children of all ages and I have to say I really enjoyed making my own as well. It's a family favourite in our house.

My children love going out to the park or the woods and collecting fallen petals and leaves, but when my son was younger he had absolutely no interest in finding pieces of nature. If this sounds familiar to you, then it's just as fun with flowers you've found in your garden, or even scraps of tissue paper cut into interesting shapes. You could use recycled tissue paper from packaging or pieces you find in craft kits. However you decide to fill your sun-catcher, the results are so beautiful. The perfect place to hang it is in a sunny window where the colour and shapes will be on show.

Materials

Kitchen foil

4 gelatine sheets

100ml water

Leaves, petals or scraps of tissue and crepe paper

1. First make a simple egg mould using foil. Draw the shape of the egg onto the centre of a piece of foil and fold the edges into place to make the egg-shaped mould.

2. Mix 4 gelatine sheets together with 100ml of water. Pour into the mould until it is roughly 5mm thick.

3. Sprinkle in fresh or dried leaves, petals and/or any scrap tissue or crepe paper you have leftover from other craft projects.

4. Press the items into the gelatine and leave to set for 2 days in the fridge. Gently peel the sun-catcher from the mould and press against a window in a sunny spot.

Continued ⟶

Decorations

Naturally dyed eggs

Continued →

Did you know you don't need to use chemical dyes to make your own beautifully dyed eggs at home? In fact, you probably even have items in your kitchen right now that will make the most stunning and vibrant colours. Onion skins, red cabbage, turmeric, beetroot and blueberries are just a few of the items that you likely have at home and that you can use to easily make a dye for not just eggs, but for many other materials as well.

I've used boiled brown eggs for my dyed eggs. White eggs will give you a vibrant pop of colour, but there's something so beautiful about the more subdued, muted colours that naturally dyed brown eggs have. These eggs are easily available here in the UK, so I've focused on finding the best natural dyes that show up well on this colour rather than the more subtle dyes that can be used on lighter-coloured eggs. If you want to keep your eggs for future decorations then you'll need to blow out the eggs as I have done with the Painted blown eggs project (see page 82). When you're using natural dyes the hard-boiled eggs can be eaten after dying. Make sure they're stored in the fridge and eat within 7 days.

Materials

12 eggs

Large pan

Sieve

Slotted spoon

Bowl of iced water

Measuring jug

Large jars

Vinegar (1 tbsp for each dye bath)

Dye ingredient suggestions

150g red cabbage

2 tbsp turmeric

8 red onion skins

2 whole beetroot

100g blueberries

Hibiscus tea

1. Put your eggs into a large pan and add water to cover. Bring to a boil, then simmer for 10 minutes. Remove the eggs using a slotted spoon and plunge into iced water for another 10 minutes before draining and storing your eggs in the fridge.

2. Gather the ingredients for each dye and add to a large pan with 1 litre of water. Bring to a boil then turn onto a low heat and cover to allow the colour from the materials to develop. The longer you heat the ingredients the more vibrant the colour will become. I recommend heating for between 30–60 minutes at the lowest temperature possible, watching to ensure the water level does not run too low.

3. Pass the liquid through a sieve into a measuring jug and allow to cool. Once cool, pour the liquid into a jar with the vinegar and add one or two of your boiled eggs. Store the jar in the fridge, checking back on the eggs every 30 minutes until you're happy with the colour.

4. Using a spoon, remove the eggs from the jar and carefully lay onto a piece of kitchen paper until dry. Store in the fridge ready to display and eat on Easter morning.

Decorations

Painted blown eggs

Decorating eggs is nothing new. In fact, it has been a way to celebrate holidays for thousands of years. These days there are quite literally hundreds of ways to decorate eggs but painting remains one of the most popular. I've embraced the springtime inspiration from my garden and stuck to a floral theme for my painted eggs. A small brush makes painting the eggs much easier.

Making blown eggs is simpler than you may think. This process means you can keep your painted eggs to reuse each year. You can also cook up the insides of the egg into a delicious omelette!

Materials

Eggs

Skewers

Paint brushes
of different sizes

Paint – 5 or 6
different colours

Pot plant or pot with rice

Straw

1. Wash your eggs then make a small hole in the top and the bottom of the egg with a sharp pointed knife.

2. Blow into one hole, until all the yolk and white of the egg has been pushed out through the other hole into a bowl set underneath.

3. Submerge the blown eggs in a bowl of water to wash out any remaining egg, then blow out the excess water as before.

4. Choose three different base colours for your eggs. I've chosen white, sage green and a deep blue. Place the egg onto a skewer using the blow hole and paint the entire egg in one of your base colours.

5. Push the other end of the skewer into some earth in the ground or a plant pot. Alternatively, fill a narrow but tall pot with rice and push the skewer in to hold it while the paint dries.

6. Once all the eggs are dry, use a small brush to paint your designs on the eggs. Don't be afraid to experiment with the shapes and colours you use. If it all goes wrong, wipe off the excess paint and cover in the base colour. Once the paint is dry, you can start again.

7. Build up layers and colours, leaving the paint to dry between coats. Once you're happy with your design, leave it to fully dry on the skewer.

Continued ⟶

Decorations

Copper Wire Egg Baskets

Continued →

What better way to display your newly decorated eggs than in a simple wire basket. The basket holds the eggs securely while also allowing the contents to shine. I've used copper wire to make these baskets and give them a pop of colour. If you prefer you can use spray paint on the wire baskets after making them, transforming them into any colour you choose.

Materials

Small dipping bowl

1 coil 2mm copper wire

Pliers

Masking tape

1 coil 0.5mm copper wire

Nail file

1. Find a small dipping bowl and turn it upside down. Measure a piece of the thicker wire that will go across the overturned bowl with a few centimetres to spare.

2. Cut three pieces of wire this length and lay them across the bottom of the bowl, equally spaced in a star shape. Tape them together at the centre, squeezing the tape into place to maintain the spacing.

3. Bend the wires over the bowl towards the lip, then bend them over into the mouth of the bowl, keeping a tight tension to hold them in place. Secure them with masking tape to stop them sliding as you weave.

4. Measure a piece of the thinner wire around the base of the bowl, add a few centimetres and cut. Wrap one end around one of your thicker wires, push it down to the lowest part of the bowl without being on the base.

5. Take the long end of the wire and take it over the top of the next spoke and then wrap it under and around the wire to secure in place. Don't wrap it so tightly it moves the spoke wire, but not too loosely it won't hold in place. Repeat until you reach the point where you started. Wrap the wire over and under the start and cut off the ends.

6. Repeat steps 4 and 5, moving up the outside of the bowl as you do. You should see the bowl beginning to take shape. Before you reach the top, remove the tape, unfold the wire and take the bowl out of the wire casing. Turn the ends of your wire into small loops with pliers.

7. Wrap another section of wire around the basket as described in steps 4 and 5, then one final time thread the wire through each of the loops made in the ends of the thicker wires in step 6. Cut off any wire ends and file down with a nail file to stop them catching.

Shredded recycled paper nests

In recent years more and more parcels are being delivered using eco-friendly packaging, which is much better for the environment. This additional paper is easy to recycle, but also a fantastic craft material.

I've used shredded paper packaging to make these Easter nests. An egg-filled nest is a classic Easter decoration that can be used to brighten up the table or as a fun way to gift chocolate eggs.

Materials

PVA glue

Paint

Shredded recycled paper

Baking paper

1. Mix half a cup of PVA glue with a tablespoon of water. Add paint to achieve the desired colour.

2. Take a small handful of shredded paper and dip it into the glue mixture. Shape it into a circle around 10cm in diameter on a sheet of baking paper.

3. Repeat this process to build up the sides and base of the nest until you're happy with the size and shape.

4. Leave the glue to fully dry then peel off the baking paper. Fill with eggs and other treats to finish.

Decorations

Spring wreath

Wreaths are not just for Christmas. In fact, the symbolism behind the wreath is to celebrate the ever-changing seasons. It's a reminder that even in the darkest depths of winter we have spring to look forward to again soon. Putting a spring wreath on your door can be a celebration of the lighter, warmer months ahead.

My personal preference for a spring wreath is something very simple and minimal. I like to add a good amount of green foliage before dotting florals around the wreath. But there are so many ways in which you can make a wreath beautiful. Decorating just part of the wreath or filling it with blooms are also stunning options. I'm going to show you how to make my favourite kind of wreath here, but don't be scared to experiment with different ideas. Each and every wreath is unique and there is no wrong or right way to do it!

I have foraged for the greenery in my wreath from my own garden and from wild spaces, but I have bought the flowers from a local florist. I've used a long, malleable branch which I have coiled and held in place with wire. This is a very inexpensive way to make a wreath base but you can always use a ready-made one available in florists.

Materials

Flexible branch
or wreath base

Thin craft wire

Green leafy stems

Flowers

Scissors

Cutting pliers

1. If you are making your base, use a large, flexible branch and wrap it into several loose circles roughly the size you would like your wreath to be and hold it in place with wire.

2. Using your green stems build up the base, weaving them into the base and occasionally wrapping with wire to hold them in place.

3. Now it's time to add the floral accents. Cut down the stems and weave them into the wire, greenery and base. Leave the flowers loose as you position them, then once you are happy with the placement, secure them with wire.

Continued $\longrightarrow$

DECORATION

Salt dough dyed decorations

Continued →

Decorations

93

Salt dough is something you can whip up from items that you will most likely have in your kitchen cabinets. It's inexpensive, easy to make and versatile. The perfect combination for crafting with children. I've made my dough even more appealing by giving it some colour. It's surprisingly easy to get vibrant, bright colours, which stay just as vivid when the dough is dry, using only gel food colouring. This is an investment, but I've had my set of gel food colours for around 8 years, using them for both baking and crafts, and I'm not even halfway through them. You can buy individual gel food colours from the supermarket, too, so they don't have to break the bank.

What I love most about this craft is the random effects that are created as you mix the different colours together. Each time the dough is rolled out for cutting gives a new look. You cannot control the effect, which leads to lots of very happy accidents.

Materials

300g flour

300g salt

250ml water

Red, orange, yellow and blue gel food colouring

Latex gloves

Baking paper

Rolling pin

Cookie cutters

Skewer

Cord

1. Preheat the oven to 120°C/100°C fan/250°F/gas 1 or the lowest heat possible.

2. Combine the flour, salt and water in a large bowl and mix until you have a soft, doughy consistency.

3. Separate the dough into five sections and add each one to a bowl. Add a drop of food colouring to each piece of dough. I left one section plain to help add some space between the colours. Mix the food colouring into the dough until the colour is consistent. I wear latex gloves to do this to avoid staining my skin.

4. Lay a piece of baking paper onto a flat surface. Break the dough into small pieces and dot them over the baking paper. Use a rolling pin to roll out the dough into one piece about 5mm thick.

5. Press cookie cutters into the dough to create shapes. Remove the excess dough. A skewer is helpful to get the clay from between the shapes. Then use the skewer to create a hole on each shape.

6. Place the baking paper onto a baking tray and put in the oven. Check every 10–15 minutes and turn them over when you can see the salt crystallise on the surface of the flour. Continue to bake for 2 hours. You can also leave these to air-dry for 24–48 hours.

7. Thread a piece of cord into each shape and tie into a knot to create a loop to hang the decoration from.

Seed mosaic decorations

Salt dough decorations aren't just good for little ones. Get older children, teens and even adults involved with making these beautiful mosaic decorations, creating unique patterns with simple ingredients.

Nature truly does give us the best inspiration. Even your home can be a treasure trove of natural objects to be creative with. The kitchen is a great place to start to find a beautiful range of shapes and colours from the most simple of objects. I've made these decorations from items I found raiding my larder. Dried beans, lentils and seeds come in a wonderful variety of colours and sizes. But if you don't have these items in your cupboards, check outside for seeds, leaves and fallen petals to use.

If you do want to give these a go with younger ones, stick to the smaller seeds and supervise throughout.

Materials

300g flour

300g salt

250ml water

Baking paper

Rolling pin

Cookie cutters

Skewer

A selection of dried beans, lentils, seeds, leaves or petals

Baking tray

Cord

1. Preheat the oven to 120°C/100°C fan/250°F/gas 1 or the lowest heat possible.

2. Combine the flour, salt and water in a large bowl and mix until you have a soft, doughy consistency.

3. Lay a piece of baking paper onto a flat surface. Use a rolling pin to roll out the dough into one piece about 5mm thick.

4. Press cookie cutters into the dough to create shapes. Remove the excess dough. A skewer is helpful to get the clay from between the shapes. Then use the skewer to create a hole on each shape.

5. Use your natural items to make patterns in the dough. Press the pieces firmly into the dough so they stay in place once it has dried.

Continued →

6. Place the baking paper onto a baking tray and put in the oven for around 2 hours. Check every 10–15 minutes and turn them over when you can see the salt crystallise on the surface of the flour. You can also leave these to air-dry for 24–48 hours.

7. Thread a piece of cord into each shape and tie into a knot to create a loop to hang the decoration from.

Embroidered card bird garland

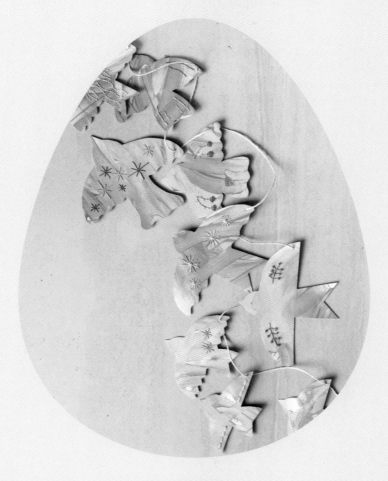

Continued →

A garland is such a festive addition to any room. When you make your own you can tailor it to fit your space perfectly, no matter how big or small. Depending on their ages and abilities, children can help you with part or all of the creation. One way I make this with my youngest is to blob paint over a large piece of card and get her to spread it around with her hands. Once it's dry you can then cut out the bird shapes, which have beautiful tonal colours.

This is also a great way to introduce slightly older ones to embroidery. Punching pre-made holes in the card to stitch into with a plastic needle is a safe and easy way for preschool children to get involved. You can find embroidery floss in high street pound shops and craft stores. Some larger supermarkets even stock them in packets of various colours. Team them with a large needle you're ready to start your embroidery.

Materials

Recycled card

Paint (optional)

Pencil

Scissors

Skewer or toothpick

Plastic or tapestry needle (which has a large eye)

Embroidery floss (thread)

Cord

1. If you want to, paint your card before cutting out the bird shapes and leave to fully dry. Lightly draw around 10 birds onto the card with a pencil and cut them out. If you want to you can create a template on paper and use this to make the birds uniform, but I prefer each bird being slightly different to the next. You can paint the birds now or leave them natural, if you prefer.

2. Using a skewer or toothpick, punch holes in a simple pattern into the card. You can use some of my patterns for inspiration. It's best to create a small area to start with and add more later if you want to.

3. Thread the needle with your embroidery floss and tie a knot at the longest end. Thread this through the back of the bird using a pre-punched hole as a guide. Continue to sew into the holes and build up a pattern. When you're happy, tie the thread up at the back.

4. When all the birds are ready, make a hole in the top with the skewer and sew a piece of cord through all of the birds to make the garland.

Play

Play

Nature bunny mask

Is there anything cuter than little ones hopping around a garden playing bunnies? These nature bunny masks are a hit in our house. It's a craft made up of two parts. Firstly we take our Easter baskets out into our garden or the park to find weeds, daisies and dropped flowers and petals. I also like to add any dried flowers I have on hand to the mix. These are usually the smaller, filler flowers that come in larger bouquets. They often outlast the bigger flowers and instead of throwing them away with the rest, I trim off the end of the stalks and leave them in a dry vase.

To make the mask I prefer a thinner cards like a cereal box. This bends easily around the face and makes the sizing much more flexible. Once I have a good shape that fits well I trace and cut out several masks, ensuring I leave one as a template for any future masks. My children love making these even more than they like wearing them, so I always make sure I save cereal boxes and thin cardboard mailers well in advance!

Continued $\longrightarrow$

Play

Materials

Recycled card

Pencil

Scissors

Cutting mat

Craft knife

PVA glue and brush

A selection of flowers, leaves and dried plants

120cm ribbon

1. Draw the shape of a rabbit's head roughly the width of your child's head onto the card and cut it out. Make the ears around half the height of the mask and give the rabbit large round cheeks. This will give the mask plenty of space for decorating. Place the mask in front of the child's face to check the fit and position of the eyes, drawing their placement with a pencil. Then place the mask onto a cutting mat and cut holes for the eyes using the craft knife.

2. Add glue to the areas of the mask you would like to decorate, using a brush or glue spreader. Add small pieces of flowers and foliage. Take care not to add too much or it will not hold in the glue. If you're making this with very small children it might be helpful to break up the greenery into confetti-sized pieces first.

3. Once you're happy with the mask, leave the glue to dry. Using the craft knife, cut a slit in the mask on both sides. Thread a piece of ribbon around 60cm long into each side. Wrap around the head of the child and tie into a bow at the back.

Cereal box egg cups

This is a really fun way to serve a boiled egg, whether you decide to decorate it on Easter morning or simply just eat it. This is especially useful if you don't have egg cups to hand, but even though we have enough egg cups for everyone in our home I like to make these with my children as a quick craft to keep them busy for 15 minutes. This also gives them a chance to have a creative burst, which is great for younger ones who don't have the longest attention span.

I've used recycled materials to make these egg cups. Cereal boxes and any paint, papers or glitter that you have stored away for crafts. It's a fun way to celebrate Easter without spending any money, by using what you already have.

Materials

A cereal box (or other recycled card)

Ruler

Scissors

Marker pen

Paint, crepe paper

Glue

1. Measure and cut out a 14 cm x 5 cm piece of card from the cereal box.

2. Measure and mark a line 1cm from one of the long sides. Use this line to help you cut a scalloped edge, cutting half circles to the line. You can use a marker pen lid to draw the half circles or just freehand them.

3. Paint and decorate the card with the crepe paper and leave to dry. Once dried, glue the edges together overlapping about 1cm to create a ring. Once the glue is dry, place your egg inside ready to decorate or eat.

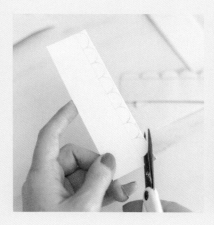

Woven egg basket

Weaving a basket from card is so much easier than it looks and it's a great craft to do together with older children. Making this project with recycled boxes means it costs nothing, as long as you have a little glue on hand, and at the same time it is good for the environment.

I really love a circular basket and I feel it's worth putting in a tiny bit more time to set up your card as a circle. If time really is a pinch then a square basket is a little bit quicker. Just follow the instructions but create a square as the base of the basket instead of a circle.

I like to paint the card before cutting and weaving, but if you don't have the time you can weave in plants and flowers once the basket has been constructed to give it a beautiful natural twist. You can personalise it by adding ribbon, handmade pom poms or paper flowers to create something truly unique.

Continued →

Materials

Recycled card
(like cereal boxes)

Pencil

Scissors or craft knife

Ruler

Hot g lue and glue gun

Strong paper clips or mini
clamps (optional)

Flowers or ribbon
(optional)

1. Draw an 18cm diameter circle into your piece of card.
   Draw 2cm strips coming out from this circle starting
   with the top then working your way around the circle.
   Cut out the strips, making sure each strip is 10cm
   or longer.

2. Fold each strip up and against the base and press the
   fold down firmly so it easily stands upright. These will
   be your spokes. Cut a 70cm x 3cm strip of card. You can
   use several pieces and glue together if necessary.
   Starting at the circular base, glue this onto the back
   of your first spoke. Hold in place with a clip or clamp,
   if available. Weave this long piece of card between
   the spokes, taking it in front of one piece and then
   behind the next. When the entire circle is finished,
   glue it into place.

3. Cut another strip of card the same size as the last and weave around the basket again, but where the last strip went on the outside of the spoke, take this strip through the inside and vice versa.

4. Fold the front spokes over the last strip of card and tuck them into the back of the card on the second row down, then glue them into place. Cut off any excess card from each back spoke and glue against the back of the basket.

5. Cut one last strip of card 50cm x 2cm for the handle. Glue to the inside of the basket at opposite ends and leave the glue to fully dry. You can now add any additional elements to your basket, like weaving in flowers or ribbon.

Play

Paper bunny bags

Continued →

This might be just about the cutest way to give an Easter gift. Like all the best craft projects it's deceptively simple to whip up and will make any gift extra special. You can use any paper bag for this project in any colour. The space in the finished bag is around half the size of the original, so make sure you start with a bag much larger than the gift or gifts you want to place inside. This is a very sweet way to gift something smaller, like a piece of jewellery. You can buy smaller paper bags and scale this down to make a mini bunny bag. So cute!

The ribbon I've used is made from cutting 2cm-wide strips of soft, drapey fabrics like chiffon, silk or viscose. I often find these in scrap bins at fabric shops and they are very easy to cut into strips to create a ribbon. You can also use more traditional ribbons that are available in haberdasheries, craft stores and gift shops. You can leave your bag plain and minimal or decorate with some sweet bunny features. Adding a pom pom or cotton ball for a tail is a quick and easy way to create a cute look. If you want to go all out, draw a rabbit face on the other side as well.

Materials

Paper bags

Pencil and scissors

Paints/pens/pom poms/
cotton wool balls
(optional)

Ribbon

1. Lay the bag on a flat surface and fold in half. Around halfway down the bag, begin to draw the bunny ears. Once you are happy with the shape, cut out the ears and unfold the bag.

2. Add a face to your bunny, if you like, by drawing or painting eyes, a nose, mouth and whiskers. Optionally, add a tail to the other side of the bag using a cotton ball or pom pom.

3. Push the bag out from the inside so it can be filled. Add your gifts, chocolate or treats to the inside of the bag. It's easier to tie up the bag if it's full, so add extra tissue paper to pad the gift out if needed. Cut a piece of ribbon longer than you need and wrap it around the bag, then tie a knot in the ribbon and pull together gently so the bag closes. Tie into a bow and cut off any excess ribbon.

Crafts

Sock bunny

A sock bunny is a very easy and very quick way to make a plush stuffed toy. They make a very sweet alternative gift from all the usual chocolate eggs and cost next to nothing to make. I make my sock bunnies a little differently to most. Instead of using the opening as the top of the head I turn the toe end into the long rabbit ears. Not only does this give you full, squishy ears but it also allows you to create a cute fluffy tail from the sock opening.

You will need a needle and thread to make this bunny. A simple mending kit that you can buy from the supermarket or most corner shops will be more than enough. The sewing is minimal and a simple running stitch – taking the thread through both sides of the fabric to create a dashed line – is sturdy enough for this project.

Materials

Women's trainer socks

Scissors

Needle and thread

Stuffing

String

Permanent and felt-tip markers

1cm wide ribbon

1. Turn the sock inside out. From the toe end cut down the middle of the sock around 5cm to create two ears.

2. Using a needle and thread, sew from the top of one ear, starting in the middle. Sew the top of the ear so it is rounded and symmetrical with the opposite side. Keep sewing along the cut edge down to the end of the slit and back up the other side.

3. Tie off the thread and turn the sock the right way around. Push stuffing into the ears, then into the rest of the body until the toy is firm and full.

4. Thread the needle again and stitch a long running stitch around the cuff of the sock. Pull this tight to gather the cuff and bring it together in a cute little tail. Tie off the thread and trim the excess.

5. Tie a piece of string around the body to separate the head from the body. Then using a permanent marker draw on the eyes, nose and mouth. Draw any additional details with felt tip markers.

6. Add a ribbon around the neck with a bow and your sock bunny is ready.

Easter wands

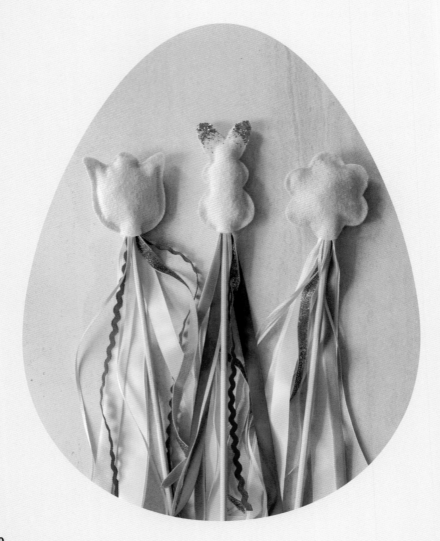

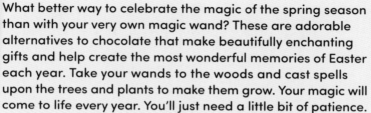

What better way to celebrate the magic of the spring season than with your very own magic wand? These are adorable alternatives to chocolate that make beautifully enchanting gifts and help create the most wonderful memories of Easter each year. Take your wands to the woods and cast spells upon the trees and plants to make them grow. Your magic will come to life every year. You'll just need a little bit of patience.

This is a no-sew craft, so it's easy and quick for anyone to complete. I've used a hot glue gun to secure the wand together. Hot glue is strong, fast and works on a range of materials, which makes it perfect for this type of project. For the handle of the wand you can use either a thin craft dowel found in craft or DIY stores or find your own from nature. Craft stores usually sell pre-cut dowel in the right size, but ones from DIY stores will need to be cut with a small saw or strong pliers.

Tailor the wands to your children's interests and passions by choosing different shapes and designs. If they love anything sparkly find some eco glitter and cover your wands in sparkles. Do they love superheroes? Give your wand a cape. Work in their favourite colours or animals and create something they know has been made just for them.

Continued ⟶

Materials

Felt sheet

Scissors

Marker pen

Glue gun and glue sticks

Stuffing

Ribbon

Stick or dowel

Tape

Glitter, sequins and other embellishments (optional)

1. Draw a simple shape onto a piece of felt around 7cm wide and tall. This could be a rabbit head, Easter egg, flower, bird or anything else you want to make. Cut out two pieces of felt in this shape.

2. Squeeze hot glue to the outer edge of one of the shapes, leaving a 1cm gap for the stick at the bottom. Press the second felt piece onto the top and wait a minute for the glue to cool and set. Push the stuffing into the gap to pad the shape.

3. Cut pieces of ribbon about 30cm long. Hold them together at the top of the stick and tape them onto the stick. Add hot glue to the top of the stick and push into the padded shape. Add more hot glue to the opening of the shape and press together to close the hole.

4. Add your choice of glitter, sequins or other embellishments with glue to decorate the wands.

Recycled wax crayons

Continued ⟶

This is not only an amazing way to make a sweet and thoughtful gift for just pennies, it's also an incredibly satisfying use for all those worn-down and broken crayons. I can never bring myself to throw away those stubby bits of crayon that no one uses anymore. So this project is one I make regularly for different seasons to give those crayons a new lease of life!

If you just happen to have an Easter silicone mould to hand you can fill the spaces with broken crayons and heat on a low temperature in the oven for 10 minutes until the wax has melted. Take the mould out of the oven – it's best to put it onto a baking tray to avoid spills – and leave to cool. Your crayons are now ready! You can sometimes find these silicone moulds or ice trays in supermarkets and pound shops, but in my opinion it's not worth spending more than a couple of pounds on this because there is another, much cheaper option.

It is very easy to build your own moulds, using what you most likely already have in your kitchen, from homemade dough. Use the recipe from my salt dough decorations project (see page 93) to create a solid block of dough. In this way you can create unique and bespoke moulds from items you find in your home.

Materials

Salt dough

Easter figures, shapes or items from around your home

Old wax crayons

Grater

Old pan

1. Take a lump of salt dough around the size of a small orange. The dough needs to be slightly wet, so add extra water by running your hands under the tap and smoothing the water over the surface of the dough. When your dough is ready, squash it into a disc about 3cm thick.

2. Take your figures or objects and press them into the dough to make moulds. Ensure there are no holes in the dough.

3. Grate your crayons and sprinkle several different coloured gratings into the mould. Melt a base colour in an old pan that you no longer use for cooking. Pour the hot wax into the mould and leave to set.

4. Once the wax has cooled enough to harden, put the mould into the fridge for 15 minutes. Take the mould out and peel off the dough. Wash off any excess dough from the crayon, dry thoroughly and your crayon is ready.

Papier-mâché egg

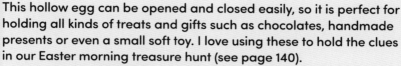

This hollow egg can be opened and closed easily, so it is perfect for holding all kinds of treats and gifts such as chocolates, handmade presents or even a small soft toy. I love using these to hold the clues in our Easter morning treasure hunt (see page 140).

For a strong egg, you'll need to create at least six layers of paper. It actually doesn't take too long to cover the balloon, but waiting for each layer to dry can be more time consuming. I like to make several eggs at the same time. That way, while I'm waiting for each egg to dry, I can be working on the next. This is also a great family craft, so get everyone making and decorating the eggs together to make the process quicker and more fun!

Continued →

Play

Materials

Recycled paper

PVA glue

Water balloons

Craft knife

Pencil

Cereal box

Paint

Coloured paper

Hole punch

1. Rip your paper into small strips and put to one side. In a small bowl pour 1 part glue to 2 parts water and mix well. Blow up the water balloon to the size you want your egg and place on a flat surface.

2. Dip the paper into the glue mixture and layer over the balloon. Repeat this process until the balloon is completely covered with six layers of paper, leaving the paper to dry between each layer.

3. Once the paper is dry, cut the balloon next to the knot. This is a great way to deflate a balloon without the bang. Add a little more papier-mâché to cover the hole. Once that is dry, use a pencil to draw a line around the centre of the egg to use as a guide. Carefully cut along this line using a craft knife.

4. Cut a strip of card 1cm thick and long enough to wrap around the egg. Glue this onto the inside of one of your egg halves, leaving a lip for the other side to slide onto.

5. Once the glue is dry, paint and decorate. I've used a hole punch to create paper confetti. Punch holes in various colourful pieces of paper and store the circles left in the bottom of the punch. Coat the egg in glue and sprinkle the confetti onto the surface of the egg, gently pressing them down with your fingers.

Handmade seed paper

What better way to celebrate the arrival of spring than with flowers or, in this case, the promise of flowers. Seed paper is such a lovely gift, especially for children. Taking time to help them put the seeds in a pot or a flower bed, giving them the responsibility to water them and seeing the wonder of nature work her magic is something money can't buy.

Seed paper is so easy to make from paper and card you have in your recycling bin. I like to use empty egg cartons; they often come in subtle colours, which helps make your seed paper look even more special. I've found the best seeds to use are wild flowers. These are easy to grow in most conditions and are always a welcome addition for pollinators in any garden.

I use a very inexpensive hand blender to make my seed paper. If you have an old blender in the back of a cupboard gathering dust you could consider using it for this project. Alternatively, you can cover your card and paper in hot water and leave it to soak for several days until it naturally breaks down into a smooth pulp. You can also use your hands or a potato masher to help work it into this consistency if you want to speed up this process.

Continued $\longrightarrow$

Materials

Egg box

Hot water

Hand blender

Sieve

1 packet of flower seeds

Towel

Scissors

1. Tear the egg box into small pieces and place in a large bowl or bucket. Pour hot water over until you have covered all the card, then leave until cool. Use a hand blender to work the card into a pulp.

2. Pour the pulp into the sieve and strain out the excess water. Transfer the wet pulp back into the empty bucket and add the flower seed. Pour all the flower seed into the pulp and mix well.

3. Lay a towel down on a flat surface. If it's a hot day I like to do this on paving stones in my garden but you can also use a bath or shower tray. Pour the pulp onto the towel and flatten down to a thin paper. A rolling pin can help spread the pulp. Leave the paper to dry, replacing the towel and flipping it over once the top of the paper has dried.

4. When the paper is dry, cut it into egg shapes. You can also write instructions onto the paper if you're giving this as a gift to friends or family.

Crafts

CHAPTER 03

Activities

Activities

As we head into the Easter holidays, finding fun activities for the entire two weeks can feel a little daunting. If the weather is on our side then there's plenty of opportunity for outdoor play, but having easy, inexpensive indoor activities to put together in a pinch can save you money on expensive trips out and at the same time create fun family memories.

Egg hunts are a classic Easter activity, but there are many more ways you can set up and incentivise a game looking for clues or prizes. Whether the game is played inside the house, in the garden or another outdoor space like the beach or woodland, we can introduce unique and interesting activities that keep children entertained for hours on end. I've included three different Easter-style hunts: a treasure hunt, a scavenger hunt and a classic Easter egg hunt, all with various challenges and rewards to offer as alternatives to chocolate.

I've included several ideas if you need a less rambunctious activity, too. Growing a cress garden is an interactive way to show how a seed transforms into a plant in a very short amount of time, and to make it even more fun I've added some cheeky rabbits to watch over the garden. When you feel like unleashing your creative side, get ready for the Easter bonnet parade or make an irresistible edible house. Make your own simple paper flowers for the spring posy stand and create a very fun animal-themed photo booth to take pictures that you can look back on for years to come.

Easter treasure hunt

Our typical Easter Sunday includes two different Easter hunts. The classic egg hunt is held by Grandma in her beautiful garden. It's something I know she loves to organise and the kids have the best time searching for eggs filled with all sorts of different treats and mini prizes. So with that to look forward to we take a different approach at home and we organise a fun little treasure hunt in the morning to look for their Easter eggs.

Materials

Cards to write clues on – make your own to add a personal touch to your hunt

8–10 clues – I've given a few examples to get you started

Easter basket or other 'treasure' for the end of the hunt

The hunt begins

At some point in the morning the Easter bunny will drop the first clue through the letter box and the treasure hunt will begin. We then run around the house solving clues that eventually lead up to the final prize. This is a great indoor alternative to an Easter egg hunt, which is typically an outdoor activity, but there's no reason you can't take this outside. If you're confident the weather will be fair then add some clues to take you into the garden. Or set up in a local park or woodland. You could even write your clues on stones and mark them with an egg or special sign for a nature treasure hunt. Make sure you write very detailed clues to help you find the next one or they might get lost forever!

Crafting clues

If you're looking for quick family craft ideas, you can turn the making of the clues into a pre-Easter art activity. When my son was little, he would not sit and paint for more than 10 seconds. He just had no interest in it. So I had to think of ways we could make things fast to pique his interest. Making our Easter egg clues was one of the more successful quick crafts we did. I squeezed plenty of paint onto a thin piece of card and got him to swish it around with a large brush. Then I quickly covered it with another piece of card and we pressed down with our hands, pushing the paint around in between the pieces. Peel off the top piece of card and you have two pieces of card covered in paint. When they're dry, cut them into egg shapes and write the clues on the back.

Continued ⟶

Setting clues

Clues don't need to be over complicated. We write simple rhymes to make it all seem that little bit more whimsical. Here are some examples of easy clues for small children:

The Easter bunny's been to visit.
This first clue was on the mat.
You'll need to find the second clue,
try looking in a hat.

Quick put this hat on!
It will help you think.
Could the next clue be hiding
in the place you get a drink?

There's nothing better than a drink
of water on a nice hot day.
Can you find your next clue hidden where
you like to play?

Rabbits like to hop around and chicks
like to go cheep cheep.
Check out where your next clue is hidden
where you go to sleep.

We write around 8–10 of these simple clues for our younger children, eventually leading to an Easter basket with a chocolate egg and a few other Easter treats. If you're looking for ways to work in alternatives to chocolate, the basket can contain crafting items, books or small toys. Alternatively, a treasure hunt can be just that, looking for treasure. Perhaps each clue could also be a piece of a jigsaw puzzle which makes a map to show where a prize is hidden. Or the clues could include a craft activity with a piece hidden with each new clue. Once all the clues are found the pieces come together to make a prize!

Scavenger hunt

Continued →

If you're looking for an alternative to the traditional, chocolate-fuelled egg hunt, why not try arranging something a little bit different? A scavenger hunt is a fun activity for all ages and can be tailored to suit anyone from toddler to adult!

Easter is a great time of year to come out of hibernation and watch the world come alive again. As soon as the days start feeling longer and you don't need to layer up to leave the house, venturing out to spend time in nature can feel like a tonic. But Easter is an unpredictable time of year. It can be the first beautifully sunny weekend of the year, or it can feel bitterly cold again. A scavenger hunt is a versatile activity that can be customised to work whatever the weather or place, and it can help children get excited about the changing seasons around them.

Materials

Scavenger hunt lists – choose from the ones I've suggested or make your own

Prize for the end (optional)

Indoor scavenger hunt ideas

A rabbit toy

Something yellow

A big spoon

Two eggs (make sure you have some boiled, wooden or plastic eggs to find)

A book with a rabbit or chicken in it

Three flowers (real, artificial or paper cutouts)

A nest for your eggs (let them use their creativity to make this)

A rabbit's tale (cotton wool)

Something with wings

A basket

Outdoor scavenger list ideas

A feather

A small bird

An egg shape

A yellow flower

Blossom

The tallest tree

Something fluffy like a lamb

A butterfly

A bunny ear shape

A duck

Activities

Make a list

Here's an example of an Easter scavenger hunt I use for my younger children. It's an easy way to get started and has a range of simple and more complicated things to find. I love adding 'things that look like' to the list, because it gets their imagination working. And while you might give prompts like, something fluffy could be a cloud, you never know what they will come up with themselves. To make your own scavenger hunt first identify objects that need to be found. For smaller children this could be just four or five items but for older ones you'll want to make things more challenging. After you have made the list, decide whether to use pictures or clues for the participants to follow. One thing I love to do with my younger children is to get them to draw their own pictures to follow.

Clues can be simple or more complex depending on your child's interests. Do they love science? Perhaps add a scientific element. For example, find something that uses photosynthesis. Simple rhymes also make fun riddles for children to solve. They don't have to be complicated or difficult to solve. It can be as simple as something like this: I stay in one place then in autumn I'm free. Find me rustling on a tree.

Take it inside

If the weather puts a dampener on your outdoor plans, give your scavenger hunt an indoor twist. Make a list of things to collect and even specify an amount to make things more interesting. Hide your items in unusual places and give clues to where they are.

Prizes

Whilst the fun is all in the activity, you could make it extra exciting by offering a prize for completing the list. This could be in the form of an egg using the 'egg-shaped object' item from the list. Perhaps using a filled papier-mâché egg with a small prize inside. The choice is yours!

Activities

Easter egg hunt

An Easter egg hunt is perhaps the most iconic Easter activity. Take a group of children, hide eggs and let the chaos ensue. Pretty simple really, or so it seems. When children are young, it's easy to encourage a fairer way of searching and sharing their finds. But if you have a number of children over different ages, the excitement can become a bit too overwhelming and it can prove more challenging to keep the activity running smoothly. I have a few tricks up my sleeve to make sure the Easter egg hunt stays fun for all and doesn't descend into the Hunger Games in your back garden.

Materials

Easter eggs or other goodies to hide and seek

Categorise

A quick and easy trick is to split your eggs into different groups. Give your eggs a distinguishing feature, be that the colour or by adding a flower, tag or ribbon to each egg to show who it's for. This way each child is looking for their own eggs and will hopefully ignore any that aren't in their group.

Team sports

Another way to ensure that the eggs are split fairly between many children is to turn the egg hunt into a team game. If you have enough willing participants, get the grown ups involved and have an adults versus children race to find the most eggs. Place two baskets on the ground to fill as the eggs are found, then at the end pool the eggs and share. You can say the winning team gets all the eggs, just make sure the adults don't win.

Continued ⟶

Activities

Relay race

Alternatively, turn the hunt into a relay race with just one, big team. Line up the children and send them out to find one egg at a time. Make a big show of timing how long it takes them to find all the eggs, which should give them some urgency and make it more exciting. At the end, everyone will come out with the same amount of eggs and there could even be a bonus prize for finding them all within a time limit. Everyone's a winner, including you!

Turning your egg hunt into a relay race also helps to extend the fun. Unless you're hiding a lot of eggs the hunt can be over pretty quickly. You can also slow things down by creating a treasure map for the eggs. Make sure your eggs are really well hidden then mark them on a simple map. For older ones this could include challenges, for example, reaching high-up eggs or finding a key to a locked box.

Alternatives to chocolate

Whichever way we decide to run the hunt, it's all about the eggs. This doesn't mean you have to overdo the chocolate. You can hide some alternatives to chocolate eggs, and even if you want to go sugar free there are so many ways to make the egg hunt special. I like to use my papier-mâché eggs (see page 126) and fill them with non-edible goodies. Handmade gifts centred around your child's interests are in many ways much more special and last longer, much longer, than chocolate does. You might be thinking that this seems like a lot of work, but making your own gifts doesn't need to be time consuming. I have some ideas in the Craft section of this book for small, handmade gifts. But you could even package up the materials and give these as a craft activity. I would have loved that as a child, but if you don't have a crafty kid there are still plenty of options for easy gifts that are inexpensive. Small wooden figures or toys made from recycled materials are becoming more mainstream and cheaper to buy. A set that can be hidden in several eggs can make a really fun and easy gift.

Animal faces
photo booth

I don't know why but my children love any peep-through boards we come across – the ones that have painted pictures of people or animals with a hole for the face. They are traditionally seen at seaside resorts and fun fairs but we find them at zoos and other tourist attractions all the time. My children love having their photos taken with these, so I thought I'd replicate the experience at home for our Easter celebrations. The benefit of this is adding more to the experience with extra props and some of my best face-painting skills. More like a photo booth really, but with a nod to the very wholesome, fun-of-the-fair vibe from generations past.

Materials

A large piece of cardboard

Thick felt-tips and paints

Props (raid the dressing-up box for these)

Scissors

Pencil

Sticky-back Velcro tabs or strips

Make the board

To make your board, find a large piece of cardboard and cut a hole big enough to easily fit a face inside. In pencil, draw an animal around the hole. Rabbits are a great choice because of the Easter theme but also because they are instantly recognisable without drawing the facial features. You don't have to be an artist to paint a simple animal. Draw long ears and round furry cheeks on your rabbit. Give the bunny big paws and a round furry body and that's all there is to it!

Dress it up

In most photo booths there's a dress-up element to make them extra fun. I was imagining the paper dolls I used to love dressing up as a child when I put this activity together. Cut out simple props to take this activity to the next level. Hats, hairstyles and accessories work well. Crowns, magic wands, tutus and shoes are just a few ideas you can create. Add some sticky-back Velcro tabs or strips to the cardboard animals and then add them to the back of your props. Now you can dress up your animals in any number of different ways before taking far too many cute photos. It will keep the kids entertained for hours and you will have the photos to remember it for years to come.

Continued ⟶

Posy flower stand

Continued $\longrightarrow$

This is quite possibly the sweetest activity I've ever set up for my children and it's one that I will be repeating every year for as long as they will let me! My children love playing shop and this way we can make thank you bouquets for all the family while we play at the same time.

Materials

Large piece of cardboard

Small boxes

Paint, paper or fabric to decorate

Scissors

Hanging pots, small vases or waste paper bins

Recycled brown paper or brown gift wrapping paper

String

Flowers or make your own with

Coloured paper

Paper straws

Glue

Make the stand

To make the stand you'll need a large piece of cardboard and some small boxes. Simply cut a large hole at the top for the window. Cut two large triangles with a slit halfway down them from the top. Cut another slit in the bottom of the large piece of cardboard that's the same size and then slide one of the triangles and the large piece of card together to allow it to stand on its own. Do this at both ends of the cardboard to give your flower stand a sturdy base that can be taken apart and stored away easily.

To make the shelf, cut a long strip of cardboard 10cm longer than the length of the window and around 10cm wide. Cut two slits on either side around 5cm long and slot them into the sides of the window. Once in place push down to the bottom of the window. Now for the fun part. Decorate your flower stand with paint, paper or by draping fabric. You could even add a chalkboard or give your stand a name. I've painted some stripes to look like a classic shop front awning and some flowers on the sides for fun. Once the stand is decorated it's time to add your flowers.

Floral delights

You can use real flowers split up from shop-bought bouquets or make your own.

I love making very simple paper flowers and I think it makes the activity even more adorable, and as a gift it lasts much longer. It's also an additional activity you can get your children involved with. These simple paper flowers are made from easy cutout shapes which are glued onto paper straws. I went all out and added paper greenery by cutting out leaf shapes and gluing them along the straw as well, which I think gives the bouquets a fuller, more thoughtful feel.

I've placed our flowers in hanging pots and cut holes in the cardboard to hang them from. You could also use small vases or waste paper bins scattered around the front of your stand. Add extra boxes to give the flowers some height for a classic florist look. When your family or friends arrive, ask them to pick out three or four flowers and some foliage for their own bouquet.

Pre-cut triangles of recycled parcel paper or brown gift wrapping paper to wrap around the chosen flowers. My five-year-old really got the hang of this after I showed him a couple of times. Then I helped him tie a piece of string around it to hold it in place and the bouquet was ready to be given. He loved giving out the flowers and our guests had a very sweet gift to take home at the end of the day.

Activities

155

Easter bonnet parade

The Easter bonnet parade is an eagerly anticipated event in our house. It's the crafting pinnacle of the year and we all make time to sit together and let the craft supplies explode around us. And while the clean up might take me longer than the activity itself, it is absolutely worth it. The rules are, there are no rules. Your hat can be a headband or a helmet or floating three inches above your head, if you can logistically make that work. It can be delicate and delightful or outrageously extravagant. Individuality is celebrated. Easter bonnets are a display of passion and personality, which makes every single one unique and interesting.

Materials

Hats

Card – if you're making your own

Glue

Scissors

Embellishments – both natural and shop bought (I used crepe paper)

Red craft felt

Lolly sticks

Prizes (optional)

If making trophies

Small rabbit figures

Small boxes

Spray paint

Bonny bonnets

If you're making an Easter bonnet for the first time, a great place to start is with a classic Easter bonnet hat and build from there. You could find second-hand hats in charity shops or use something you have hiding in the back of a wardrobe. Supermarkets now sell Easter hats ready for decorating in the build up to Easter, to give you a head start, or you can even make your own. A simple top hat made from card is easy to put together. Firstly create an oval rim for the hat. The inside diameter should fit comfortably on top of your head. Then cut a large piece of card just slightly longer than this measurement and add tabs along the length. Glue the tabs to the rim and secure the ends together overlapping that extra few centimetres. Now you have a simple hat to build your bonnet on. Once you've chosen your preferred headwear, it's time to start adding the embellishments.

Continued →

Activities

This is where it gets interesting and your personality can shine using ready made embellishments or making your own. My passions are obviously crafting and also nature. I love floral accents, so I've based my hat on those aspects of my personality. Your hat will be a celebration of all things you, so let your imagination shine through and if all else fails add lots of Easter eggs, chicks and rabbit ears to make a bonnet you will be proud to show off in your family parade.

Time to parade

Once you have finished decorating your bonnets it's time to roll out the red carpet and showcase all the creativity. You don't need a literal red carpet, but a roll of red craft felt is a fun way to recreate your very own catwalk to strut your stuff on. There are no winners or losers in the Easter bonnet parade but it can be fun to rate each effort and give out prizes. Make your own score paddles with large ice lolly sticks and card circles to give scores or make scorecards rating the creativity, colour, silliness or even the most eggs. You can create your categories once the bonnets have been finished to ensure everyone wins a small prize. These could be chocolate bunnies, certificates or you could make your own trophies. Superglue a small rabbit figure to a box and cover both with spray paint. Write your categories on the trophies and reuse year after year to create a tradition they will cherish.

Cress bunny garden

Continued →

One thing that is in abundance around Easter is the humble egg box. A staple in any crafting stash and something most people have on hand or can rummage in the recycling bin for. I've turned one of the many empty egg boxes I have in my home into a cress garden. What makes this special? Well, we have two rabbit gardeners to watch over this veg patch. And for once they won't be eating it all!

This is a very easy activity to get the whole family involved in. From making the rabbits to sprinkling and watering the seeds, this mini garden is sure to foster an interest in how food is grown.

Materials

Egg box	Cotton wool balls
Scissors	Packet of cress seeds
Fine felt-tip	2 ice lolly sticks
Coloured paper, crayons or paint (optional)	

Prep the garden

To get started, cut off the top of the egg box and draw four rabbit ears onto the flat section on the lid. Cut these out and stick them onto the top of the tall spires that keep the eggs separated. I've added some additional paper to give the ears some detail, which I think is an adorable added extra. You can leave your ears plain or add the detail in crayon or paint if you prefer. Draw the eyes, nose and mouth of the rabbit. Then add any additional details such as a fluffy tail, blushed cheeks or whiskers. This is the time to get creative. I've also added a little sign to our cress garden made from things I've found in our crafting cupboard.

Sowing seeds

Once the glue has dried, add a ball of cotton wool that has been soaked in water to each egg section. Sprinkle the cress seed liberally over the cotton wool. Spritz with water every day until the cress has grown.

Once the cress is tall and ready to harvest, ask the children to mow the lawn with a pair of scissors, or if they're younger they can simply pick the cress with their fingers.

Activities

Easter edible house decorating

Continued ⟶

I've borrowed this activity from our Christmas list, but it's one that always goes down so well over the festive period and keeps everyone sitting still in one place for a surprisingly long time. With that in mind I thought we might be able to make decorating a gingerbread house work, albeit in a slightly different way, for Easter. Rather than baking the base for this house from scratch I wanted to use something ready made and convenient, just to make life that little bit easier.

Pop Tarts are the perfect snack for creating your house. They are easily cut into shape without crumbling, but are also strong enough to hold the shape of the house. The colours are more light and vibrant than the darker gingerbread, which makes it feel more spring-like from the start.

Materials

Pop Tarts

Royal icing

Sharp knife

Piping bag

Brightly coloured sweets

Construct

You'll need royal icing for the 'glue'. I have a simple vegan royal icing recipe that will work perfectly for this on page 36. To build the house, take two Pop Tarts and cut them to a point on one of the shorter sides. Do this with a sharp knife, cutting from the centre of the longer side to the centre of the shorter side. Do the same on the opposite side to create a classic house shape. These are the front and the back of the house. Cut another Pop Tart in half to make the sides and use the royal icing to glue all of these pieces together. Take two more Pop Tarts for the roof and glue these into place. Now your sweet little house is ready to decorate.

Decorate

The premise for decorating your house is the same as a gingerbread house: use brightly coloured sweets to add the detail. The icing works well in a piping bag, which helps control where and how much you use, but for smaller hands it is easier to use a bowl to dip your accents into before adding them on. If you're unsure how to decorate your edible house, start by creating roof tiles with smaller pieces and elaborate doors and windows. You can cut or crush sweets and snacks to make them fit or use them whole. There are no rules, so enjoy the fun of it all before snacking on your house later.

Activities

Styling

Styling

There's a notable shift around Easter when the light from the sun becomes warmer and brighter. It's one of my favourite moments of the year, when all of a sudden my home feels more fresh and cheerful. At this time of year I'm drawn to using brighter colours in my decor, adding accents wherever I can. I don't mean painting a whole room or buying new furniture. It can be as simple as a new tablecloth or placing a handmade wreath on the door.

I do like to dedicate a few spaces to my home for seasonal decorations. My favourite is decorating a mantel. The fireplace is usually a focal point in a room and has a lot of styling opportunities. There is space on the mantel itself for placing objects or hanging garlands and there's also room on the floor around it for larger objects. It gives us a lot of options to explore with our Easter decor.

If you have less space in your home, then a simple basket can provide a perfect spot for adding the Easter spirit. Not only is it compact but it is also portable so it can be placed in different areas. They also make great gifts for others or just as a treat for yourself!

It's not just indoor styling. A few simple pieces can make the most of your outdoor space whether you have a large garden to enjoy or just a small balcony. Brightening up this space and using it to its full potential is incredibly restorative after spending a lot of time indoors over the winter months. It might not quite be the time of year for balmy summer evenings yet, but there are often bright and cheerful days that are pleasant enough to enjoy a coffee or maybe even an alfresco lunch.

Easter mantel

Styling a mantel is a wonderful way to bring an occasion into focus in your home. Your mantel is usually at the centre of a living area, which will draw the eye naturally. Adding a little extra festive styling will help your home feel welcoming and make the Easter holiday feel more special.

Materials

Paper

Ribbon

Glue gun

Large decorative items

Candles

Foam board

Paint

Papier-mâché eggs (see page 126)

Bunting

One way to instantly add that party feeling to your home is bunting. There's a reason bunting has stood the test of time. It never fails to make life a little brighter and can be used just about anywhere, inside and out. This paper bunting is quick to whip up and has a big impact. You can use recycled papers, magazine pages or wrapping paper to make your bunting eco friendly.

To make your bunting, fold a rectangle of paper into a concertina then, holding the folded paper together as a strip, fold it in half. Glue the pieces together where they meet and fan the rest out to create a semi-circular fan. Use hot glue to attach the straight edge to a piece of ribbon. Repeat this with all your paper to make quick, colourful bunting.

Continued →

Styling

Structure

Styling the mantel shelf is all about creating areas of varying height. An easy way to create a vignette that is pleasing to the eye is to think about your mantel in terms of one large triangle. Start with something large in the centre to bring the height to the triangle. This could be a mirror, picture frame or even decorative items such as large woven plates. This could sit on the mantel or be attached to the wall. You can also use several pieces that overlap, which works well with picture frames in particular, layering smaller items in front of a focal piece. Once the central items are in place you want to create two smaller triangles at either side. These triangles do not have to be symmetrical or even the same size but it does help to think of the collection as a triangular shape. Group together a collection of three to five objects with varying heights, shapes and colours to help guide the eye and keep the look homely and natural.

Candles add height, but can also give a pop of colour and with it a spring vibe. I've used floral candle holders for a fun twist that also bring a cohesive colourway. Adding floral accents or potted plants gives your mantel warmth with a touch of nature. At this time of year the new season brings us such a welcome change from the barren cold of winter. I've embraced the bloom of spring as the theme for the mantel adding floral decorations from top to bottom.

Finishing touches

Easter is all about the magic of spring, so to give my mantel a whimsical touch I've made these very easy oversized flowers. Draw a flower onto a piece of foam board and cut it out with a craft knife. Paint the flower and glue a small stand to the back using a triangular piece of foam board from the offcuts, so it can stand on its own. This is a very inexpensive and easy way to create a big impact on a small budget.

As this is Easter I felt the mantel needed something a little extra. These papier-mâché eggs make a great finishing touch. You can paint them in a colour to bring the theme together or decorate them more ornately to add some pattern to your mantel.

Easter dining
table

Continued →

The dining table is one of my favourite places to bring spring colours into my home. If you're usually more reserved with colour or don't know where to start, adding some accent pieces in bright pastel colours will make any space feel fresher and give it an Easter vibe. Mixing pastels is an easy way to create a cohesive look using colour. Depending on your taste you can go for a minimal look with pops of colour or a maximalist style by flooding the table with colour. This look is beautifully bold and vibrant but if you prefer something more low-key then pair the colour with softer neutrals to keep the tone calm.

Materials

Candles

Wax crayons

Grater

Flowers (real, artificial, paper or a mix of all three)

Painted blown eggs (see page 82)

Napkins

Vases and jars

Pink, blue and yellow gel food colouring

PVA glue

Colour

Candles are an inexpensive way to add colour. But if you don't want to buy new candles you can easily update your white candles to make them more colourful. Melt candle wax in a bowl over a pan of hot water. You can use any leftover candle wax or cut the bottom off your taper candles. Grate in coloured wax crayons until you have the desired colour, then dip your candles into the wax. Dip several times to build up the colour. This adds a wonderful pop of colour for next to nothing!

Flowers

Adding flowers to any table brings a breath of fresh air. They create a feeling of new life, especially in the spring. Whether you choose real flowers, artificial or paper flowers, pick bright colours in tulips, daffodils and daisies and add sparingly, scattered in several vases to really show off the blooms.

Setting the scene

There are lots of other ways to DIY fun, festive decor while spending very little. I've created these cute place settings using my painted blown eggs (see page 82) and napkins I already owned to make the bunny ears. To turn your napkins into cute bunny ears, fold the napkin in half from corner to corner to make a triangle. Fold a 2cm strip from the long edge and continue to fold over until you reach the corner. Wrap this around the egg and tie the two ends together on the other side of the egg with a piece of string. Fluff out the ends to make ears and place them on each plate. These whimsical decorations bring an element of fun to your table without breaking the bank.

Pop of colour

Another way to add colour without spending money is dying old or inexpensive vases or even jars with food colouring. You can do this with food colouring and PVA glue. Combine 1 teaspoon of water, 5 drops of gel food colouring and 2 teaspoons of PVA glue in a bowl and paint it onto the inside of the glass. Turn the vase upside down to allow the excess to drip out onto some scrap paper and leave to dry. Unfortunately adding water to this vase will wash away the colour but it's a beautiful way to display artificial or paper flowers.

Styling

Easter tree

An Easter tree is a wonderful addition to your home over the holiday season. Unlike a Christmas tree, the Easter tree is a smaller, more subtle offering made from a simple branch or collection of branches to create a table-top display. It is a beautiful, natural way to display your homemade decorations and celebrate the start of the season. But while placing a branch in a vase sounds pretty simple, taking a moment to consider a few of the design elements can help your tree shine.

Materials

A large branch or a few smaller branches

Vase

Rice

Sticky tape

White paint

Shape

Firstly you'll need to pick your foliage. If I can, I like to prune back a branch of the neighbours' plum tree that hangs over into our garden. If the timing is right the blossom is in full bloom and the branch looks stunning simply placed in a vase with water.

Foraging

But you don't need a garden teeming with blossom trees to create a beautiful display. In my local park the gardeners will prune and cut off any dead branches throughout the year. I usually find a pile waiting for me to take my pick. If you live near a forest or woodland, you will have your pick of fallen branches to choose from. (Remember to check the rules of managed parks beforehand.) When you've found your branch, fill a large vase with rice and position it in place.

Clean lines

If you're struggling to find the perfect branch, consider using a number of long, straight branches. Use sticky tape to create a grid pattern over the top of the vase and place your branches through the holes created to spread them evenly.

If you want to give your tree a cleaner, brighter look then try painting the branches white with either spray paint or a household emulsion paint.

Styling

175

Front door

I love giving my home an Easter makeover, but spring styling is not limited to the interior of your home. I'm going to show you a few quick and easy ways to transform your front door to create a warm and inviting entrance that will be sure to make everyone who sees it smile. Let your front door be the focal point of your home, as guests are greeted by a whimsical arrangement of wreaths, spring-inspired garlands and floral accents.

When you're styling an exterior, quite often less is more. You don't need to give your door giant bunny ears to create an Easter vibe. You can be a little more subtle, adding a few simple touches to celebrate the season and some colourful accents for spring that will brighten up the front of your home.

Continued $\longrightarrow$

Materials

Wreath

Door mat

Pencil

Marker pen

Sponge brush

Hanging baskets and potted plants

Papier-mâché eggs (see page 126)

Balance

The first thing that every spring door needs is a wreath. A wreath is a traditional sign of celebrating the seasons. The circle aspect represents the years flowing into each other, with spring bringing new life after the sparse winter. It's also something you can tailor to your own personal tastes and ideas. You can use foraged flowers on a simple coiled twig (see page 90) or glue blown eggs (see page 82) to a foam wreath base. You can weave beautiful blooms into a rattan wreath or use felt or paper to create handmade floral arrangements. Your imagination is the only thing that limits you! No matter which style you choose, wreath making is an activity that helps you to slow down. It gives you the opportunity to take a moment for yourself in something creative and almost meditative. When finished, place your wreath in the centre of your door and enjoy it every time you come home.

Welcoming

Another way to make coming home even more enjoyable is a decorated doormat. It's a very easy way to add a fun element to your seasonal door styling. I have painted bunny ears into our mat. It took about ten minutes using my children's poster paint and a sponge brush. You can draw out your design in marker pen first, or if you're feeling confident, go straight in with the paint. You could paint flowers, Easter eggs or even a welcome greeting on your mat. The choice is yours!

Colour

One of the quickest and in my opinion most effective ways to create a welcoming front door is to add plants. You can do this with hanging baskets or by placing plants in pots around the door. Florals will brighten up any door and grasses in pots create large areas of colour without being overwhelming. To give these plants a little extra Easter fun, add your papier-mâché eggs (see page 126) to the baskets to give them pops of colour and make your guests feel as if they're walking into an Easter wonderland.

Easter baskets – 3 different styles

Continued ⟶

As with many other holiday celebrations, the pressure is on parents to make Easter more special every year. Have your children had as many chocolate eggs as their friends? Did you have the big days out making memories? It can sometimes feel less about celebrating the time of year together as a family and more about keeping up with everyone else.

But instead of bombarding them with chocolate and treats to make the time feel special, I work the day around easy activities and fun we can have at home. In the morning we hold the Easter treasure hunt (see page 140) and the prize at the end of the hunt is an Easter basket full of fun. Yes, there's a chocolate egg in the basket, but there are also games, crafts and handmade presents that we can use as a family to make those memories on a much smaller budget.

I love putting this basket together every year and I'll admit, I might enjoy the aesthetic more than the children do at this point, but either way it's always a really fun surprise to find at the end of our treasure hunt.

Upcycled wooden crate

Materials

Wooden crate or small box

Shredded paper

Recycled paper and card

Scissors

Cord

Toothpick

Blu Tack or tape

Two sticks or long skewers (optional)

I have a few of these wooden crates around my house and I have to admit one year when I was short on time I tipped out the contents and quickly filled it with shredded paper and a few little bits for the end of the Easter treasure hunt. And of course my son did not notice the difference and was just excited to find his Easter crate. Once he was done pulling everything out of the crate I emptied the paper and refilled it with its original contents. Easy, quick, low cost and sustainable. This is a great option if you're looking to save time and don't want to buy additional filler for your celebrations, especially as it doesn't need to be a wooden crate. You can use any small box you have in your home, even a cardboard box that you can make that little bit more special using things found around your house.

One inexpensive way to decorate the box in minutes is paper bunting (see page 169). It's such a simple idea that I love and use all the time. Use recycled paper and card and cut them into triangles. If I can get away with it I like to use my children's old paintings that are destined for the recycling box. Make holes in two corners with a toothpick, skewer or sharp scissors and thread a piece of cord through. Either add your bunting to the box with Blu Tack or tape or use two sticks or long skewers to dangle the bunting above the contents of the box.

Wicker basket

Materials

Wicker basket
....
Tea towel or small piece of fabric
....
Decorations (optional)
....
Ribbon
....

A classic wicker basket is such a beautiful way to display your gifts. It's easy to drape a tea towel or small piece of fabric inside to arrange the gifts over. Place the larger items at the back and reduce the size as you move towards the front. If you can, try to fill the basket with the gifts. But if you do have space left once everything is in place, add decorations such as wooden eggs, dyed boiled eggs (see page 79) or even a few carrots from your fridge to fill up the empty space while keeping on theme.

If you want to keep the basket simple, you're done. But you can also take the basket to the next level by adding additional decorative elements.

Wrapping ribbon around the handle or threading it through holes in the wicker can add a beautiful pop of colour, which is also useful if you're making several baskets for different children. Give each basket a different colour ribbon for each child. If your basket is at the end of a treasure hunt, tie a piece of the same colour ribbon on the clues to guide the children to their own basket. Alternatively, you could do the same thing with flowers or plants. Or you might want to add a label to the basket with their name on to make it very clear who the basket belongs to.

Styling

Recycled card bunny basket

Materials

Recycled card

Woven egg basket (see page 110)

Paint or pens

Scissors

Glue

If you have a bit of extra time and you want to make something really special that can be used for years to come, you can weave your own bunny basket using recycled card. You can find a detailed tutorial on how to build the basic basket in the Craft section of this book (see page 110). Once you have your basket it's time to add the extras.

Cut two long pieces of card with a rounded point at the top to look like rabbit ears. Using paint or pens, add a pink arch to the ear and then weave or glue the ears into the inside of the basket. Cut out the details for the face from the leftover card and paint black. Glue these onto the front of the basket and your little bunny is ready. Fill the baskets with your treats and enjoy seeing their little faces when they find it!

Easter garden styling

If we're lucky Easter Sunday falls on the first warm, sunny weekend of the year where you can physically feel the shift in the seasons. There's nothing like welcoming in the spring by spending every possible moment soaking up the sunshine, going for long walks and relaxing in any outdoor space surrounded by nature. It's also a really nice weekend to give your garden, balcony or patio a quick refresh. Tidying up just a small area to enjoy over the bank holiday doesn't have to take over the whole weekend. A few quick additions can turn a rundown space into a spring oasis.

Continued ⟶

Materials

Herbs

Evergreen plants

Pots

Paint

Tablecloths and blankets

Cushions

Outdoor rug

Basket

Vases

Flowers

Chalk

Papier-mâché eggs (see page 126)

Festoon lights

Greenery

Spring is a great time to create a herb garden. Hopefully the coldest weather is over and you can keep your herbs thriving until winter. I like to put my herbs in pots so they can be moved somewhere more sheltered, if needed. Other plants that will have an immediate impact are ornamental grasses, box hedge, ivy and other evergreens. A base of lush green is perfect for any early flowering plants to sit against, creating an outdoor space that is full of life.

Revitalise

If you can, paint any furniture that has been left out over the winter. This might seem like a big job but a quick sand and coat of paint can make a huge difference to the space. If you don't have the time or spare paint to hand, cover worn pieces with tablecloths and blankets. Adding soft furnishings like these, as well as cushions and outdoor rugs, can take a space from feeling cold and sparse to warm and welcoming. Once your table is ready, fill a basket with vases full of flowers for a stunning centrepiece that takes minutes to make.

Childish wonder

You can add a few magical touches to your outdoor space to make it feel more inviting to children. One very easy addition is drawing chalk bunny feet on the ground. This takes minutes but will fill them with joy as they hop along the feet and follow them to see where they lead. Line this path with plant pots and papier-mâché eggs (see page 126). You could even have some garden games for them to play, giving you a moment's peace to enjoy all your hard work!

In spring the evenings are starting to get lighter, but a few lights can make a huge difference to the mood as the sun goes down. Festoon lights make any space look more festive. Festoon originally referred to the garlands and wreaths that hung at festivities. Hanging these lights in a loose swag gives the space a wonderful soft glow and provides that final touch that brings it all together.

About the author

Francesca is an award-winning blogger and creative business owner making her home more beautiful with a DIY attitude. She has always believed in combining craft with design to create something that is beautifully handmade, and this ethos is a recurring theme throughout her blog, Fall For DIY. Sharing her ideas and skills with her online following of over half a million is Francesca's passion, and it is the driving force behind her continuously experimenting with techniques both old and new. Francesca's work has been featured in many print and online publications including *Elle Decoration*, *Design*Sponge*, *Mollie Makes*, *Domino* and *Apartment Therapy*.

Recipe Index

Index Of Crafts, Activites And Styling

Pop Press an imprint of Ebury Publishing,
20 Vauxhall Bridge Road,
London SW1V 2SA

Pop Press is part of the Penguin Random House
group of companieswhose addresses can be found
at global.penguinrandomhouse.com

First published by Pop Press in 2024
www.penguin.co.uk

A CIP catalogue record for this book is available from
the British Library

Design: Evi-O.Studio | Emi Chiba & Susan Le
Text & photography: Francesca Stone

ISBN 9781529924718

Colour origination by Altaimage Ltd, London
Printed and bound in Turkey by Elma Basim

The authorised representative in the EEA is Penguin
Random House Ireland, Morrison Chambers, 32 Nassau
Street, Dublin D02 YH68

MIX
Paper | Supporting
responsible forestry
FSC® C018179
www.fsc.org